DIMA'S
DOG SCHOOL

DIMA'S
DOG SCHOOL

Dima Yeremenko

& Emily Randolph

PIATKUS

bsite!

lling fiction and
nd, body & spirit,
paranormal.

If you want to:

- read descriptions of our popular titles
- buy our books over the Internet
- take advantage of our special offers
- enter our monthly competition
- learn more about your favourite Piatkus authors

VISIT OUR WEBSITE AT: www.piatkus.co.uk

Copyright © 2004 by Dima Yeremenko and Emily Randolph

First published in 2004 by
Piatkus Books Ltd
5 Windmill Street
London W1T 2JA
e-mail: info@piatkus.co.uk

The moral right of the author has been asserted

*A catalogue record for this book is
available from the British Library*

ISBN 0 7499 2506 X

Typeset by e-Digital

Printed and bound in Great Britain by Biddles Ltd,
King's Lynn, Norfolk
www.biddles.co.uk

Our faithful companions leave us behind one day, causing us so much suffering and pain. But, looking back, we wouldn't think twice about getting another dog. Without a dog, a home is not a home.

This book has been written for all the dogs in all our lives, so that every single one may have the love and happy life they deserve.

CONTENTS

Off-piste Afghan, Doushman.

PREFACE

Yesterday I was a dog. Today I'm a dog. Tomorrow I'll
probably still be a dog. Sigh. There's so little hope for advancement.
Snoopy

A great deal of research has been conducted on the art of dog training and as a result there are many resources to draw on. But unfortunately a lot of these can be very confusing to someone first embarking on dog training. My desire in this book has been to bring together all the important tried-and-tested methods and mix them with my own personal experience and methods to develop a comprehensive but very accessible and fun way to teach dog training. I hope you'll find that my most valuable contribution is our Hand Feeding method, a completely unique approach that is essential to creating the proper training spirit in your dog.

What this book offers in total is, I believe, a method of training that will give you all the tools you require to solve your individual issues and, at the same time, open your mind to the many creative solutions you can adopt to tackle your dog's particular problems. In other words, it has been specially made for you.

I've been successfully teaching the methods explained in this book through my dog centres, SIRIUS in the Ukraine and the Good Boy Dog School in Britain, and I'm delighted you've joined our extended family of trainees. Welcome, and may you soon see the infinite rewards of becoming a good trainer and teaching your dog how to be a good boy or girl. I look forward to working with you and your dog and hope you experience as much pleasure as I do every day communicating with man's and woman's best friend.

Indy the model Great Dane.

INTRODUCTION

The Origins of the Good Boy Dog School

Dima, his wife Anna, and baby Kyrill at home with a few of their pals.

My experience with my first dog, at least in the beginning, was much like that of those who don't know much about the canine kingdom. I got Jerry, an Irish setter, when I was 13. I named him after the hero of Jack London's books *Jerry of the Islands* and *Michael, Brother of Jerry.*

At the time, my mother and I lived in a flat in Kharkov, the city in the Ukraine where I was born in 1970. I'd had the odd goldfish, a few hamsters. Together with my grandfather, who kept pigeons, I'd find injured birds and nurse them back to health, setting them free when they were strong enough to fly once more. But I always longed for a dog. Like so many children, I found my nagging finally paid off when my mother thought I was old enough to handle the responsibility. Little did she know what she'd started. The care and training of dogs has been my lifelong passion from the day Jerry walked through my door.

Before the collapse of the Soviet Union, a large organisation called the Society for the Support of the Army, Aviation and Navy controlled the breeding of dogs, as well as all aspects of licensing. All dogs had to be trained to a high standard so that they could be recalled for the purposes of the military if required – even if your breed of choice was a chihuahua, a dog with no obvious military use unless you wanted him to bite your enemy's ankles!

It was a monopoly, of course, but it had its virtues. For one, it thoroughly evaluated all prospective dog owners. An inspector came to your home to see if you had enough time and money and the right living conditions to keep a dog responsibly. If you passed this evaluation, you then had to attend a dog ownership responsibility class that included everything about dogs from obedience training to anatomy and physiology. If you passed this, you were permitted to have a dog and were referred to one of the national Kennel Club's breeders for your desired breed, and would be put on a waiting list.

In those days it cost at least three months' wages to purchase a puppy, a huge sum, and a decision not to be entered into lightly – that was the point, of course. The Kennel Club also regulated prices, so any breeder who tried to charge more could lose their breeding licence as well as their Club membership. Dog ownership was not something decided on a whim. In the former Soviet Union it was easier to get married than to get a puppy.

Then, when you finally got your puppy home, you had to attend further classes taking from six to nine months (and attendance was compulsory, so that you could be graded). The obedience exam included some 27 standard off-the-lead commands that you and your dog, no matter how big or small, had to demonstrate in order for you to pass. If you didn't, you had to start all over again and keep at it until you did.

The Ukraine, and indeed the whole of the Soviet Union, had a tradition where if you wanted a dog, you also wanted to breed and show him. In fact, in the whole time I was training dogs in the Ukraine I heard of only two dogs that had been castrated. Great pride was taken in breeding and showing, and without this rigorous course work and licensing you could do neither with your dog.

Understandably, this entire procedure weeded out those who really shouldn't be dog owners. It was a tough, painstaking process, but in the end incredibly satisfying for owner and dog alike. Both felt they had a role to play, a job, and this built a wonderful bond of communication and affection between them.

Not surprisingly, we had no rescue centres in the Soviet Union; there was little need. Puppies were highly treasured and were either given to a family member to look after or sold to the best possible person. They were rarely abandoned and left on the street, and even then, many with a soft heart would care for, feed and comfort them. Because of this, I had only vaguely heard of dog shelters in other countries and was very saddened when I moved to Britain and learned of the large number of abandoned and abused animals.

Jerry was one year old when I got him through a friend who knew I wanted an English red cocker spaniel but who knew nothing about dogs. My friend described the dog to me over the phone. Long ears, red – that's all he said. It sounded like the dog I was looking for, and it came at the right time. He had been raised as a hunting dog, lived on a farm and was making a nuisance of himself killing chickens and the farmer couldn't cope. Would we be willing to take him on? The answer was an unequivocal yes!

Imagine my surprise when I found the dog wasn't a cocker spaniel but a gigantic, one-year-old Irish setter! I collapsed in fits of laughter over the obvious blunder, but in the end we decided to keep the dog even though we knew nothing of the breed. We quickly discovered he had no house manners to speak of, and we lived in a rather unsuitable place for such a large and active creature – a sixth-floor flat in a nine-storey building with no garden.

A few days after we got Jerry I left him at home while we ran some errands. Somehow he managed to slip the safety bolt on the inside of the door and lock us out. We had to go through someone's apartment on the seventh floor and work our way back down through a window. When we finally got back in, we found the place covered with flakes. Jerry had scratched all the paint and insulation off the front door and it was scattered like a blanket of snow around the flat. I was so miserable I cried. I thought my mother would never let me keep Jerry after he'd caused so much damage.

And that wasn't all. I had to take him out several times a day because we didn't have a garden. He pulled like mad on the lead, and I couldn't let him off because he was so badly behaved. A couple of times he did get away from me and ran off. On one occasion he was stolen and held for ransom. What could we do but pay up?

My mother drew the line and said that I should either give Jerry away or train him, which I would have to do anyway if I was going to keep him. So off I went every Sunday to training classes.

The Kennel Club classes each had about 20–30 people and my local group was very friendly. We all walked our dogs together and Jerry and I progressed, bonding because we spent so much time together. We had a very strict and harsh instructor who pushed us to work very hard and was very exacting. Not having had any previous experience, I found it incredibly difficult training Jerry. I always felt embarrassed, as if Jerry and I were really the worst in our group. It wasn't until about a year after I started training him that I was approached at a dog show by another training instructor. He told me he had been watching me and thought I'd make a great addition to his display team. Would I like to join him?

As you can imagine, I was thrilled. All my hard work was finally recognised. I wasn't the embarrassment I thought I was. It was quite an honour to be asked to join the team, and I have everyone who helped me with my first uneasy steps to thank for recognising my passion and pushing me ahead.

Casper, the rescue lurcher, napping between training sessions.

I took all the courses I could and graduated from the instructors' and dog-judging course at the Kennel Club before I was 15. I continued taking classes and showing Jerry all over the country. It wasn't long before he was the star of our travelling show and even won the prestigious honour of the Championship of the Ukraine.

The display team was a real school of skills. Even though there was no money in it, our little group attracted about 15 people aged between 15 and 45 with dogs that were not just reliable but able to professionally entertain a crowd.

It was up to us to create ways to impress people. Some of the dogs demonstrated their athleticism by jumping over ten dogs standing side by side or jumping rope. One dog did a routine where he carried a dumb bell, both ends flaming, in his mouth. We acted out little comical scenes and impressive military scenarios with real explosives, as well as protective work. My dog worked our distant control routine blindfold and even mastered blind search and retrieve. He loved the challenge. Among other stunts, I taught him to perform with a treat in his mouth that he had to release at the end of his act, and to climb a vertical ladder.

It was with my display team that I learned just how important it is to have a dog that looks forward to working with you. During the next few years I had the privilege of learning from some wonderful handlers and professional trainers and saw how the dogs responded to them. I wanted to 'speak Dog' the way they did. And better.

When I was 17 I was asked to instruct my first obedience group for the Kennel Club. I was very busy going to university full-time, but soon my group became one of largest training units in the city. I loved training, and I guess my enthusiasm showed because my group became very popular. I began doing some private work, and opened my own dog centre, SIRIUS. We started a newsletter, had a fortnightly TV programme and set up a small business manufacturing doggie products of all sorts.

By the time I was 25 I had reached the highest level, the national category of show judging, for which there were only 21 judges in the whole country. I judged the top championships in the Ukraine as well as in the neighbouring republics.

In 1992 I finished university and started work on a PhD, but with perestroika well under way and the Soviet Union no more, the Kennel Club disintegrated along with most of the state institutions. Sadly, there were no longer any large international dog events or even seminars to speak of. I could have carried on training in the Ukraine, but I felt I needed a bigger challenge and a better opportunity to learn more.

So many of the dog training books I've read over the years, and so many of the top trainers and behaviourists, come out of Britain and the USA, so I decided to study in Britain on a three-year PhD course in the School of Animal and Microbial Sciences at Reading University and continue my canine education. In the end, though, after a gap year that I took to prepare for the courses, I decided not to continue my studies. Hands-on work, I realised, was really what I preferred to the theoretical approach, so I decided to stay in Britain and began training dogs, establishing my own school. The Good Boy Dog School opened for business in 1996.

I remember with great fondness and pride the first dog I trained in Britain. He was an 18-month-old Bernese mountain dog by the name of Benson who'd had a few incidents involving the owners' and other people's children. I put Benson and his owner, Maggie, through a rigorous 15-week course covering most disciplinary issues, 50 various skills and a large number of self-made commands. Benson improved enormously, his difficulties with children now a thing of the past. I've bumped into him a few times since then, once outside the tennis courts at Mill Hill in London, where his owner plays sometimes. Told to go to bed, without a lead, he displayed the calmest and most confident of waiting skills. Another time he was strolling by while I was doing a training class. He confirmed my theory that old dogs remember, by demonstrating a series of advanced tricks he hadn't done in ages.

One of my next cases was an 18-month-old German shepherd named Wolf who had savagely ripped the arm of a neighbour. Wolf's owners came to me for training after the subsequent court case, as this was their last chance to keep him. They rarely walked him, and when they did, he lunged at everything. Wolf was one of my greatest early challenges, but in the end we were able to enter him into some competition classes. He could have easily become another sorry statistic.

This just goes to show that there are no lost causes. Any healthy dog can be trained, re-educated and rehabilitated. The training techniques I've developed have been tested over 16 years of work with every kind of dog and will work for any breed or any cross-breed, of any age, regardless of background.

I wish I could claim that I've written a book that gives the answers to all the many questions about training a dog. I would love to tell you that I've developed a magic wand that will turn your dog – however good or bad he is – into your dream pet or Cruft's obedience winner. But, instead, this book is a personal approach based on what has proved to work at my Good Boy Dog School. It will require a bit of time and effort on your part to develop a strong communication between you and your dog. But, in the end, I know you'll be richly rewarded with a happy, well-behaved dog you can be proud to walk in the park and in the street, take to visit friends or relatives or simply enjoy at home, just you and your faithful companion. To make it up to you for all your hard work and devotion to your dog, I promise that both of you will have a great time training and will enjoy the many benefits for years to come.

There are a number of popular books on dog training that show how to push your dog into a sit, to yank the lead to stop him pulling and to make him give up that tennis ball. These books are fine – all dogs require some training in order to fit in with their owners' lives (not the other way around) – but they neglect to address the root causes of problems.

This book suggests a different method entirely. I'll teach you how to speak Dog by helping you to understand why dogs behave the way they do and what causes some of their worst behavioural problems. I'll also show you what you are doing to perpetuate your dog's bad habits. In this way we can work together to engage your dog in a dialogue rather than giving him orders. Together we will give your dog a reason to listen to you. We will communicate with him by teaching him to think positively and to act in a pleasing manner. In other words, to be good!

Overall, this book is about responsible dog ownership. We have too many dogs being abandoned, too many dog owners who don't understand the time, patience and responsibility involved when they get a puppy or a rescue dog from a shelter. We have far too many incidents of bad dog behaviour leading to national headlines that tarnish the reputation of the dignified canine. It's our fault, not the dogs'. It's we who don't know any better. If I had my way, people would be thoroughly evaluated and licensed before they could own a dog. You're reading this book, so I know you care. I'm glad. We need more people like you.

Mackie, a rescue dog who found a loving home.

This book has enabled me to reach many more people than I would have in my daily practice at the School, and so gives me the privileged opportunity to enhance the lives of many more dogs. It allows me to show people the great fun and personal value of pet ownership. I can now be in more places than one and share with pet owners the vital aspects of training that I've learned in my many years of experience. I hope you'll find this book valuable and that it will change the way you think about dog ownership.

I'm so fortunate to live in Britain, which is a unique place when it comes to dogs. It's hard to go anywhere without meeting bunches of much-loved dogs out for the day with their owners. I'm even more fortunate to work in Hampstead and the neighbouring villages, where there must be more dogs per capita than anywhere else in the world. Every day I walk my charges on Hampstead Heath or the Heath Extension and I'm almost always accompanied by friends and clients who want to drop by for a walk and a chat, to discuss their latest challenges or to celebrate their most recent successes with their dogs. I wish you could come along too. You're warmly invited! But if you can't join me, I hope this book will guide you through this most wonderful time in your life when you're building a deep and lasting bond with your dog.

Note from Emily Randolph

Julia

I think I can safely give the credit to Julia, my Jack Russell, for the makings of this book, for if it hadn't been for her and her incredibly bad behaviour, I would never have met Dima.

The fateful day was in March 2002, by the ponds on Hampstead Heath. In the distance I saw a sight to behold: a tall man effortlessly orchestrating over a dozen dogs, all entirely off the lead and fully under control. The dogs danced around him like butterflies, light and happy, looking to him for their next cue. I'd never seen anything like it, and I knew at that moment that I'd finally found hope for Julia and me.

I'd spent the last six years trying to come to grips with my tyrannical terrier – called 'Princess Julia' by all who knew her. I'd made several unfortunate choices in trainers over the years and, on top of that, my husband and I had moved internationally several times, making it difficult for me to focus on solving Julia's behavioural problems. She even had to endure quarantine, which she did, to my surprise, with no trouble at all. I like to think my visits several times a week were helpful, but probably it was her tenacious personality that was her saving grace. Anyway, excuses aside, I was tired of trying to manage Julia's plethora of problems. I wanted to solve as many of them as I could.

I knew when we settled finally in Hampstead – a place beautifully brimming with dogs frolicking about on the 790-acre Heath and lazing on the pavement in the village while their owners sip cappuccinos – that I'd need to do something, and fast. Otherwise, I feared, we'd soon be exiled to the infamous night-walkers' club, whose reluctant membership consists solely of people whose dogs are just too dangerous to be out in the light of day and mix with the good dogs.

Although Dima didn't believe me when I approached him and told him of Julia's frenzied attacks on numerous hapless dogs – she'd put on a most persuasive show of cute, sweet and harmless on the day of introduction – she soon showed her true colours by attempting to set about a dog that was innocently walking by. So our training with Dima began in earnest, and I was soon learning about everything I was doing wrong. And all along, I'd been blaming poor little Julia!

I come from a long line of dog spoilers, and no one in my family ever trained a dog. We always thought it pointless. 'We don't want a perfect dog,' we'd say. 'We don't want to ruin his character!' But one of the most crucial things I've learned from Dima is that training isn't about creating a perfectly controlled robotic creature devoid of personality. Instead, it is about building a better relationship between you and your dog, opening up paths of communication, enjoying being together, and becoming a responsible dog owner in every way. And yes, all this, and your dog's fun-loving nature, will be left well intact. As a matter of fact, it will be enhanced, for a well-trained dog is a confident, secure dog that has understood the boundaries you've set and is therefore much more likely to be good and to be rewarded.

Julia had multiple problems, from poor social behaviour with other dogs to bad recall; jumping up on people; throwing herself into prams to lick babies (luckily for me, she never succeeded, but the desire was there); inviting herself to picnics; and biting people she thought deserving for whatever reason. I had a lot of work to do, especially as Julia was an adult dog, and her unsociable behaviour well ingrained (and all my fault). But, I'm very happy to report, you can teach an old dog new tricks – and a lot more than that – if you're willing to change your bad habits and routines.

I've tried the majority of the training techniques presented in this book, including many of the very clever technological training aids available on the market today. Julia and I have been willing guinea pigs and because of the results we've achieved I feel very confident in advocating Dima's training methods. He has given me the tools I require to address, solve and manage Julia's behavioural problems and to train in a way that is both adaptable and creative – one that is custom-tailored for me and my dog. As you'll discover later, Julia and I aren't perfect – either of us – but that's not our aim; we train to enjoy each other, to spend time together interacting, to build a stronger bond.

Dima saved us from the banished night-walkers. In fact, Julia and I are out every day enjoying all the parks around Hampstead, socialising and making new friends – just as it should be. Our communication and understanding of each other grow daily and I love her even more utterly, ridiculously, madly because of it. I've learned how to keep her safe and enable her to enjoy her life to the full – and to have fun myself in the process. I know you want exactly the same for your dog.

I hope my collaboration on this book has made it all the more accessible to complete novices and soft touches such as myself, as well as to those who wish to learn the proper groundwork for professional dog handling. I know you'll be helped by Dima's approach and the lives of you and your dog will be greatly enriched.

There are several, very important people and pooches whom I would like to thank for their support in the making of this book. First, my beloved husband, Markus, for his ceaseless devotion, good humour, optimism and support – you make it all worthwhile, my love. To Princess Julia, who always knows when it's time for me to leave my computer and take me for a walk: I know you have my best interests at heart...

Thank you, Mom and Dad, for your constant flow of well wishes filling up the electronic highway. Your enthusiasm is boundless and appreciated more than you'll ever know.

Thank you also to my favourite non-dog people who have made an exception for Julia: Sharon and Geoffrey – better neighbours, friends and cheerleaders I couldn't wish for. Thank you for all your support and sustenance!

And finally to Pepi – if I knew then all that I know now. Thank you, Whitney, Resa, Emily and Stuart, for taking him in and giving him your love.

Pepi

Enjoy, and happy training to all of you, the new students of the Good Boy Dog School. You're in for a wonderful lifelong adventure.

PART 1
DOGS AND THEIR OWNERS

Aristotle posing for the camera.

Chapter 1
Our Role in Our Dogs' Lives

Nuances of a House Dog

The dog is not allowed in the house.
OK, the dog is allowed in the house, but only in certain rooms.
The dog is allowed in all rooms, but has to stay off the furniture.
The dog can get on the old furniture only.
Fine, the dog is allowed on all the furniture, but is not allowed to sleep
with the humans on the bed.
OK, the dog is allowed on the bed, but only by invitation.
The dog can sleep on the bed whenever he wants, but not under the covers.
The dog can sleep under the covers by invitation only.
The dog can sleep under the covers every night.
Humans must ask permission to sleep under the covers with the dog.

Are you really a dog person? Perhaps you're better off enjoying your friends' and relatives' dogs, instead.

Are you really a 'dog person'? This sounds like such an inane question, doesn't it? I mean, here you are, you own a dog or are about to get one, and you're reading this book. Of course you're a dog person! But I'm going to be brutally honest. I can't tell you how many people I know who have dogs but shouldn't be dog owners. Not knowing anything about dogs isn't the worst sin of all. Many people are simply not responsible enough or haven't appreciated what a commitment pet ownership truly is. And I think many of the dog charities and rescue centres agree as they see the consequences of our irresponsibility every day in the large numbers of mistreated, abused and abandoned dogs they receive.

Recently the Blue Cross charity in Britain did a study which found that the incidence of people giving up their pets because they couldn't manage or didn't have time for them had doubled over the past ten years. The study reveals that escalating work burdens and family pressures result in hundreds of pets being abandoned when they no longer fit in with their owner's lifestyle. Just over a quarter (26%) of dog owners who gave their dogs up to the Blue Cross to be re-homed in 2001 stated being 'out all day', 'no time for animal' and 'can't cope with animal' as reasons for no longer being able to keep their pet.

Steve Goody, head of companion-animal welfare at the Blue Cross, said: 'Sadly these figures reflect modern times. Longer working hours and other pressures mean that people have less time to devote to their pets, leaving them at home on their own for long periods. Sadly it is the pet that suffers…'

Sarah Mawhinney, Press Officer of the Royal Society for the Prevention of Cruelty to Animals (RSPCA), says there are many reasons why dogs are abandoned and given up to shelters but the 'fundamental reason is probably that people haven't thought of the long-term responsibility… Quite often it can be an impulse buy and then, when the novelty wears off, that's when people want to offload an animal to a rescue centre. Sometimes there are genuine reasons, but often it does come down to the fact that not enough thought was given to the long-term lifestyle change that will occur.'

A recent article in the *Sunday Times* reported that both dogs and cats were becoming victims of divorce, with one RSPCA centre reporting that 50% of their dogs came to them as a direct result of broken homes. Jackie Ballard, director-general of the RSPCA, stated: 'For people who break up, the pet, like the furniture, is no longer an integral part of the relationship and is no longer wanted. But pets are a responsibility that you can't just get rid of when you are bored.'

Just because you melt at the sight of a puppy, it doesn't mean you'd be a good dog owner. As I've said, dog ownership requires a lot of responsibility and if you aren't up to the task, maybe owning a dog isn't for you; enjoy the company of your friends' and relatives' dogs instead.

Well socialised dogs can fit into any social situation, making life happier and easier for all.

Have You Got What It Takes to Be a Good Trainer?

In my experience, dog ownership is a little like a job: you need certain qualities in order to be good at it. The ideal characteristics include balance, composure and patience; persistence; and ambition and initiative. You also need to be precise and consistent; have common sense and be logical; be organised; and have the ability and the desire to be in control. Finally, you need enough time to work with your dog, and – it should go without saying – you need to be affectionate and loving.

Let's look more closely at these vital qualities:

Balance, composure and patience

Back in the 18th century the French writer and gun-dog trainer Robert Dommage said that the ideal dog handler isn't the kind of person who, with the appropriate training, could become, say, a chemist, but someone whose mental flexibility makes him temperamentally well balanced in the overall performance of the task in hand. I couldn't agree more. If you have a short temper, for instance, you aren't going to be a very sympathetic or effective trainer. On the other hand, a patient person will achieve excellent results.

Patience is a gift. This is what gives you inner calm and composure. In training, the patient person is one who doesn't rush ahead, but takes the time to repeat, or even reconsider, his techniques, reverse or change procedure, intensify or revise a routine. A patient person may take a long time to achieve the desired outcome, but he always seems to get there in the end and be more knowledgeable because of his experience along the way.

Furthermore, if you're patient in your training, you're more likely to learn more about how your dog reacts. The more information you can glean from him, the better you can tailor your training so that you can work with him in the best possible way.

Of course, there are quicker ways to train a dog, like using a pinch, spike or electric shock collar. I'll say more about this topic later, though such items are banned in Britain, if not in other places, like the USA. Although I've never used one nor would ever recommend one, I accept that a shock collar, employed in the proper fashion, will very quickly get rid of an undesired behaviour, such as scavenging. But why not use a gentler approach for man's best friend? A slower, more careful approach will achieve the same result and will leave the dog wanting to learn more.

A patient and composed person will also be willing to look harder for the right approach to use with dogs whose temperaments lie at the extreme ends of the spectrum; for instance, dogs that are either very timid or overconfident and too assertive. Opposing your dog's behaviour, battling him every step of the way, won't bring you any closer to victory. Instead, a patient person will learn how many repetitions his dog will need to learn something new and how intense the stimulation required. He'll play on the dog's side, to encourage and work with him to solve a task. A good dog owner plays for the same team as his dog. You're the captain, and he is your willing team mate.

Persistence

You can achieve any goal if you're persistent. An indifferent, unmotivated attitude will lead to failure, no matter what your target.

Training can't be effectively executed by half measures, otherwise you'll get an *almost* trained dog. For those of you who say, 'That's OK, I don't need a perfect dog,' I respond that *training isn't about perfection; it is about building a willingness in your dog to follow your instructions*. If you ask your dog to sit but he doesn't, and you just stand there asking him to sit over and over again, he'll be learning from you that when you say sit, you don't really mean it. This is why many dogs act perfectly well with their professional trainers and are less behaviourally consistent at home. The trainer is persistently following through with their commands while the owner is letting things slide at home. I confess to sometimes doing it myself. But if one of my pupils runs up to a passer-by in the park for some attention, I slap my own wrist and take the dog back to kinder-garten to reinforce the sequence of proper training: instruction – correct behaviour – reward.

You need to be persistent to train and solve problems with your dog and to practise repetitions as part of that training. Repetition is a vital part of dog training. Training a dog, with its language so different from ours, can be very challenging, especially if it has a troubled background. If you're willing to stick it out, if you're prepared to take on challenges, come what may, and be creative in finding solutions, you'll be richly rewarded.

Ambition and initiative

It's terribly sad to see a dog passed around like some unwanted thing, simply because people haven't appreciated all that is required to be a responsible dog owner and a good trainer. To learn how to handle your dog, it isn't enough just to show up to classes. You need both the ambition and the initiative to train and practise on your own.

Just the other day I heard a troubling but all too common story about a toy poodle, Noodles, a very cute and frisky dog that never made it all the way to becoming obedient and reliable. He had the capacity to do so, as I could see during our one-to-one sessions together, but I kept hearing from the owners that he simply refused to comply with many of the instructions his family gave him.

One day, when Noodles was less than a year old, his family went on holiday and left him with a colleague of mine, a professional dog minder, as they had done several times before. On their return they simply neglected to collect him. When my colleague confronted them, they told her to keep Noodles; he wasn't wanted any longer.

Sadly, you hear stories like this all the time. I suspect Noodles's former family wanted to be able to wave a magic wand rather than have to put any effort into following through with their lessons. Training isn't magic and there are no gimmicks, no matter what some books may claim.

Precision and consistency

It is essential, when you set out to train a dog, that you be precise in your commands and corrections. The more precise you are, the better your dog will understand what you're asking of him. *The precision of your training lies in the precision of your instructions.*

In the same vein, consistency is also crucial. If you aren't consistent in your messages to your dog, he won't understand you. If you don't want him to get up on the sofa but only tell him to get off on Tuesdays and Fridays, even though you catch him doing it every day, he won't understand that you don't want him on the sofa *ever*. If, on the other hand, you make sure every day that he doesn't get on the sofa, he'll eventually get the message.

Common sense and logic

Although it does help to be smarter than your dog, more useful attributes are common sense and logic. It doesn't matter how strong-willed your dog is, if you can be one step ahead of him and able to offer a logical response to his behaviour, you'll have a much better chance of making him understand you. Logical people are able to fashion effective strategies and tactics and make improvements to them as they go along – valuable skills in dog training.

Also, common sense and logic can be better than experience, so don't be put off by your lack of know-how with dogs. My academic supervisor back home was a professor of the physiology of behaviour. She was the owner of a Newfoundland whose behaviour was so poor that she would have needed to be brought right back to the beginning in order to train him properly. My professor could never explain to me why, despite all her deep and wide knowledge on the topic, she could not train her dog.

On the other hand, there are first-timers who easily launch a puppy to competition stardom or bring up and rehabilitate a rescue dog to everyone's envy. Sometimes the most unexpected people can be the best dog owners. Take Linda and her decision to take on a puppy...

CUBA

When it all started, Cuba wasn't even two months old. Her owner, Linda, was a complete novice. In fact, she'd always been afraid of dogs. But her son, Christian, was desperate for a dog. He had come walking with us several times and even helped us put together some photos for our website. So Linda agreed to take on the challenge. They decided on a Labrador, Cuba, who is a black beauty with a shiny wave of hair running down the middle of her back.

The best approach when taking on a puppy – and an adult dog too – is to learn as much as you can before the new arrival comes home to you. In this way you'll be less likely to get stuck later about what to do and how to resolve any problems that arise. And this is exactly what Linda did. She tried to have a class with me a week before the arrival of Cuba, who had been selected by the whole family at an earlier stage from an acceptable breeder. I was fully booked at the time and couldn't meet Linda for a few weeks, so I put her in touch with Sue Evans, a wonderful and professional trainer who runs training classes in Finsbury Park, London, for the Kennel Club of Great Britain. Sue visited Linda and prepared her well for Cuba's impending arrival, answering all her preliminary questions. I, in turn, visited Cuba two days later to set her up for her future development.

Linda worked quite a lot with Cuba and, at four and a half months, Cuba has already grasped many key concepts. She comes to Linda when there are lots of other dogs around her. A 'spy' informed me she saw Linda call Cuba out from the centre of a large group of frolicking dogs. And it wasn't a fluke. Linda did it several times and Cuba came to her every time at her first command. Amazing! Already Cuba has learned that Linda and Christian are her source of food and are even more fun than any group of playing dogs.

Within days of her arrival Cuba was 100% house-trained and behaved immaculately indoors. How many dog owners can claim the same results? Outdoors, Cuba now adores swimming and retrieving. My Hand Feeding method has also helped Cuba (and Linda) to master such skills as 'sit', 'down', 'no', walking to heel, staying and rejecting food on command, and she's very amenable to being brushed, groomed and handled. She has now embarked on learning lots of tricks, much to the enjoyment of everyone. Some of Cuba's reactions aren't reliable enough yet, but what do you expect from pup not yet five months old? She's an example for all.

Being organised

As 'Tools of the Trade' (p. 40) explains in more detail, you need to be organised in your use of training gear. But the need for this quality goes much deeper than that. In my experience, a person who runs a sloppy business, for instance, won't make a good trainer because his disorganisation most likely runs throughout every aspect of his life. If you can never find anything, the chances of your remembering to bring rewards for your dog or all the other paraphernalia required, or even recalling which pocket you've put everything in, will make it very hard for you to train your dog.

Control

Another critical quality in a good dog trainer is the ability and the desire to be in control. Many behavioural problems in dogs develop simply because people are unwilling to take control – be ruler of the roost, king of their domain, or whatever you want to call it. For instance, if your dog snaps at you every time you go near him when he's luxuriating on your favourite armchair, you aren't ruler of your universe. He is! This is all a matter of control. (To learn more about this topic, and how to apply control tactics, see 'Gentle leaders versus dictators', p. 178.)

Time

Clearly, you have to have time to spend with your dog. Each dog needs time to form future good habits and right reactions. When a new dog arrives in your home he won't automatically know what's expected of him. He isn't pre-programmed to blend in harmoniously with your life. Just as parents need time to cope with their new babies and spend years educating them, we and our dogs need time to adjust and learn about each other. A dog crèche or minder can help in many ways, but in the end it has to be you who is there for your dog.

Formal training isn't always what's needed. There are plenty of owners who have beautifully behaved dogs yet have never been to a training class in their lives. What are they doing right? They have taken the time to be with their dogs and instruct them on a daily basis. They have learned how to understand and to communicate with their dog from day one, even if they didn't even realise they were doing it.

If you go out to work all day and leave your dog at home all alone, you don't have the time he needs. You aren't being responsible. At my school we refer to such unfortunate pets as 'weekend dogs'. Their owners only have time to exercise them at the weekend, so the dogs are manic by the time they are given a bit of freedom. The dog of a client of mine was recently attacked by a weekend dog – she has puncture wounds to her neck to prove it – and many of my clients won't walk their dogs in the park at the weekend for fear of such dogs. These poor animals are just too unreliable, and their owners simply don't know what they're doing. Dogs need routine physical and mental exercise and plenty of play time – not once a week but daily.

If you work all day, please give your dog to a friend, family member or a dog walker every day. It's the least you should do. You can't expect to have a well-behaved dog if he's starved of physical and social activity.

Love and affection

Most importantly, you have to have a love of working with your dog, as well as great love for your dog himself. There will be no other reason for you to want to train him – not money, fame or prestige. Love makes good trainers better and helps a raw novice develop into a devoted trainer. Love is our primary, all-important motivation. With a little more love, there would be no uncaring and filthy puppy farms and people would not abandon their pets.

Anna and Rex have a cuddle.

Whether you know it yet or not, it is love that's made you read this book. It will be love that will help you work a little harder with your dog, to work through the challenges of training. It is love that will help you to become a better teacher to your dog. It is love that will make you enjoy more and value the gift of having a doting, gentle and considerate dog.

ALFIE

A collie-schnauzer cross-breed, Alfie was adopted from the RSPCA centre where I run rehabilitation classes for new owners of RSPCA rescue dogs. Alfie and his new owner, Bernard, trained with me until Bernard was pleased with Alfie's obedience level, calmness and reliability. They continue to train together for pleasure and always seem so happy interacting. Bernard, a young man of 83, often gives Alfie ten signals at once for him to perform in one single routine. Alfie seems to relish the challenge, and is quick to comprehend and successfully complete any task asked of him.

However, because of his age, Bernard isn't that consistent in the delivery of his commands, and so one might imagine that Alfie would have a good chance of misunderstanding him. Strangely enough, this isn't the case. They are just so tuned in to each other that no other aiding mechanism is required. Bernard has spent so much time and lavished so much love on Alfie that they have established a bond of understanding and their own way to communicate.

There is undoubtedly some form of language, though not in the sense that we normally use the term, that links humans and dogs, as they have remained our trusted and devoted companions and helpmates for thousands of years. The fact that there is some kind of communication between you and your pet brings him closer to you, bonds you and makes you feel a bit like a member of their species who can understand and converse well when communication is required.

It is understood that non-verbal communication represents the majority of our communication, and it has recently been established that dogs are supremely sensitive to our social cues - even more so than the chimpanzee, our nearest cousin in intelligence. This ability has enabled dogs to fit in with human society and has been shown to have evolved directly through genetic adaptation that 'allows dogs to enter into a new ecological niche - that of being symbiotic with people'. This hypothesis was tested by Brian Hare of Harvard University when he travelled to New Guinea to compare the reactions of a wild dog breed called 'singing dogs' to that of our domesticated dogs. Singing dogs, even ones that had been reared by humans, were no better than chimpanzees at gauging people's non-verbal signals. Therefore, it is the genetic adaptation of our domesticated dogs that has led to their greater understanding our social cues. ('Dog Behaviour: Sensitive Souls', *The Economist*, Feb. 2004.)

Monty Roberts, widely known as the 'horse whisperer', after his book *The Man Who Listens to Horses*, came up with a new language, Equus, which is what horses use to communicate with one another. When you learn about an animal and let it learn about you, you develop a very special language that the two of you can use whenever you decide to have a 'chat'. Invite others to share the experience with you and let your dog learn to understand others. Your communication with your dog may then grow at a steadier and swifter pace. Forget about teaching your dog to be your bodyguard. Invest in an alarm instead and enjoy the company of the new member of human society: your pet.

I've talked about the qualities and outlook you'll need if you are to succeed in training your dog. But you're probably aware that there are also plenty of gadgets on the market – even if some are useless and many even dangerous – to help you deal with your dog's behavioural issues. For just about any problem you can think of there is a device to help you solve it. It is wonderful to be aware of all these inventions, as many of them are indeed invaluable to anyone training their dog. But if all this sophisticated equipment is on offer, why does dog training require all those various personal qualities we looked at earlier?

As I explained earlier, if you want to know how your dog learns and where he gets all his good habits and clever ways, you need to spend some time first learning everything you wish him to be by the time he is mature. Whether he's a puppy, older dog or rescue dog, you need to plan ahead and map out how you wish to develop and educate him.

Are you good at chess? If so, you know how important it is to play not one but many steps ahead of your partner. In our case we're playing for the same team, but when you enter the game your wisdom will help you grasp the rules. When a new dog enters our life we want to teach them what their new life will be like from that moment on. Give them boundaries and direction. You may have owned a dog before, but just because your last dog didn't develop any bad habits, don't assume that your new one is immune. Every dog is different, and it is up to us to be prepared for every eventuality so that naughty behaviour doesn't become habit. Fill your dog's life with good things, rewarding experiences and lots of love and guidance. *Teach him what to do instead of what not to do.*

If you want to get to the root of your dog's problems and solve them for good, I don't recommend relying solely on any techno-logical device. This isn't to say that the technology available today, like citronella anti-bark collars and ultrasonic repellents, can't aid us in training, but it isn't the overall answer. Admittedly, properly addressing a behavioural problem isn't the easy way, and it takes time and dedication. That said, it is extremely fulfilling when you overcome an issue through proper training. It is one of the most rewarding experiences you can have with your dog.

After explaining our core training method, we look in the final chapter at a wide range of 'management solutions' to dogs' behavioural problems, many of which use modern training tools. However, it is imperative that you already have good training skills to be able to use these tools to best effect; and it is best always to use them as supplements, not substitutes. Even then, to use this equipment in the proper fashion, you may need to seek hands-on guidance from a professional trainer. The instructions given with many such products are inadequate.

However, if all you want is a quick fix, to put a sticking plaster on the problem, so to speak, and you manage to achieve this, then training isn't for you; and neither is this book.

Nor is this book for you if you feel that the pharmaceutical companies have all the answers to your dog's behavioural problems. Nowadays many owners ask their vets for drugs such as Prozac or Clomicalm for their dogs. In my opinion, drugs are too often prescribed for issues that can be managed and solved through training. Although there are instances where medication is the only solution, why anyone would choose to use drugs rather than the healthier options is beyond me. I can only think they must be getting very poor advice or looking for a quick way out of a problem.

Many drugs have very nasty side effects, and long-term use may cause additional medical problems. Should the question of drug treatment for your dog arise, your best defence is to arm yourself with as much information as you can in order that you can make an informed decision.

Chapter 2
How Dogs Think and Learn

Why, that dog is practically a Phi Beta Kappa. She can sit up, beg,
and she can give her paw – I don't say she will, but she can.
Dorothy Parker (1893–1967)

Just like other higher mammals, dogs don't just respond to stimulation automatically without conscious reflection. Their responses aren't always habitual, built up from past experiences and performed unconsciously. Dogs, like us, do have expectations and formulate theories. They can, for instance, build a mental map of events or places and take themselves from one point to another even if they have never been shown the direct route. Because of this, a great part of our training at the Good Boy Dog School is designed specifically to release this kind of mental energy within your dog and to teach him how to use his mind to its full potential: to add up all the information he receives, to estimate his chances and to anticipate the consequences of his actions.

Line up, guys. It's lesson time!

Dogs are also very like us emotionally. All creatures feel pain, stress, excitement, love and even loss. But it is often the case that we believe that our dog's motivations and actions are all human too. I disagree. Dogs don't chew up your sofa because you didn't take them out on their favourite walk and have ice cream like you promised. They don't pull on the lead because they're angry with you and want to wrench your back out. They don't wee on your newly laid white carpet because you forgot it was their birthday. Their actions and motivations are much more natural and innocent. To project human motivations on to them – in particular resentment or revenge – is unfair and inaccurate, and won't help you communicate effectively with your dog. There is a lot of truth in US actress Martha Scott's observation, 'Do not make the mistake of treating your dogs like humans or they will treat you like dogs.'

Although they will never speak our language with its complicated syntax, structure and grammar, dogs can learn quite a lot about what we need from them if we first learn about how they think and learn, and, second, if we know how to teach them our wishes in a way that they will understand.

Until we understand how to speak Dog, as I'll teach you in this book, we humans are going to have problems communicating right from wrong to our dogs. We will continue to see dogs abandoned, and otherwise healthy dogs destroyed – all because we just didn't understand them and they us. Assuredly, your dog deserves better. And this is where I can help.

I'll show you a very simple model of how dogs react and how their brains work. Many devoted scientists have spent their lives coming up with models that explain such activity, and for you to be familiar with the basics will help you be a better trainer. We're responsible for the good health and happiness of our dogs, and we're responsible as well for their safety and the safety of those who come in contact with them. Only proper training can accomplish this and it is filled with lifelong rewards.

Why Do Dogs Do the Things They Do?

Now, I won't bore you with a dissertation full of theories; there are plenty of excellent books covering animal behaviour and psychology (see Bibliography, p. 252). However, the more you understand about how your dog thinks and learns, the easier it will be for you to work successfully with him, and there are a number of elementary things you need to know before you begin training your dog.

Beauty in a traffic cone.

Medical problems

Occasionally there are medical reasons why a dog is exhibiting bad behaviour. He may even be in pain and acting up because of it. Before starting any training programme, have your dog carefully examined by a vet to ensure he is healthy. It goes without saying that it is inhumane, as well as futile, to attempt to train an injured or sick dog.

Dogs with knotted hair or skin and coat problems may also be affected emotionally by their condition. So be sure to keep their exterior, including their eyes, ears, paws and claws, in peak condition. Get professional advice on body weight and development as many aspects of a dog's behaviour are closely dependent on these.

Don't, however, let yourself become obsessed with or over-reliant on the medication that some vets prescribe for anxiety and distress, as many problems are behavioural and therefore better treated by a behaviourist or trainer. A good vet will guide you in the right direction.

Motivation

The precursor for training a dog is finding out what motivates him. Dogs have many chemically conditioned needs for many things, including air, food, water, sleep, comfort, affection, exercise, sex, parenthood, security and emergency, freedom and exploration. Most of their behaviour is directed at satisfying these needs, or motivators, which are common to all dogs. However, as individuals dogs also have their own personal drives, and these vary in intensity from dog to dog. This variation is seen in the strength of emotions such as fear and anger; in traits such as dominance and sociability; in issues of self-image such as strength of ego and obsessions; and in interests such as ball playing and bone chewing.

Dogs are the same in the wild as they are in your own home; it's just that in the wild they have to satisfy their own needs. At home you are your dog's sole provider. Where food, above all, is concerned, this idea is exceptionally important to a dog. For you as owner, food is not just the easiest motivator to administer to your dog, it is also the most reliable and logical tool you can employ when working with him. The training technique I teach means you'll communicate and reinforce the idea that you're the main provider of food, thereby making it easier to train your dog with treats – a wonderful reward for his pleasing behaviour. It is also essential that you train yourself to comfortably juggle between the use of various kinds of rewards, like treats, toys, play time and a bit of off-lead freedom, as we're going to use all these to achieve the best results. It's like hiring your dog to do a job for you and paying him handsomely for successfully executing it – in dog currency.

Contrary to popular belief, dogs are particularly motivated by food rather than by the desire to please you. Jean Donaldson, in her book *The Culture Clash*, thoroughly squashes this misconception. 'Generations of dogs have been labelled lemons for requiring actual motivation when all along, they were normal.' Your dog isn't doing anything for you; he is 'completely and innocently selfish'. For various reasons, not the least of which is that we like to humanise our dogs, we've been very uncomfortable with this knowledge and have long blamed our dogs for being stubborn or even vengeful. We're imposing human morals on them when in reality they aren't so sophisticated. They are dogs, wonderful in their own right.

We shouldn't be disappointed that they need a bit of motivation to do something. Just look in the mirror. Couldn't you say the same about yourself? Even people who selflessly do volunteer work are doing it, in part, because it makes them feel good or fulfilled.

Lack of knowledge

Many dogs have never been taught the difference between what is and what isn't acceptable to human and canine society. To a dog, all of his behaviour is fine. It's up to us to let him know what we think is good and what is bad. It sounds obvious but it's amazing how many of us assume our dogs already know, or should know, what we expect of them.

Misinformation

A large degree of undesirable dog behaviour is caused by owners giving inconsistent or mixed signals to convey commands. If you aren't consistent in your use of signals, they will be flawed and mis-understood by your dog. The stronger and more efficient the signal you give your dog, the stronger and more reliable his response.

Good training is first and foremost about you learning how to be a good teacher. It is about learning how to effectively broadcast your wishes in the clearest fashion to your dog.

Socialisation

Dogs are highly social creatures by nature but, because of the busy lifestyles of their owners, many haven't been properly socialised with people, children and other dogs. Without proper socialisation *under supervision*, dogs don't learn how to properly communicate with other dogs (in ways deemed acceptable to humans), nor do they know what is expected of them when they are around people.

Peppi, Dennis, Bonnie, Mac and Trixie having a quiet sit-down.

When left to their own devices, dogs in a wild pack will sort out their own social behaviour as it suits them. But this behaviour may not be acceptable to us humans with whom they cohabit. They need clear and precise directions in order to follow human society's rules and to meet our own personal expectations of what we feel is appropriate behaviour. (You can read more about socialisation in 'Step 4: Active Socialisation Under Supervision', p. 154.)

Unhelpful instincts

Encounter in the park.

There are a number of canine instincts that can make training a dog very challenging: dominance, protection, possessiveness, hunting and sex, to name a few. That's why it's so important to master the basic training skills I teach in this book; in this way we can overcome these unhelpful instincts or at least divert them to suit our sensibilities. Do you want your dog humping everything in sight? Of course not: it's embarrassing and generally not welcome by other dogs and their owners. Do you want your dog chasing after every cat? No, of course not, especially if one day he might follow it across a busy road. The tools I equip you with will help you to inhibit the instincts you find disagreeable. The skills needed to manage and control them may even be needed one day to save your dog's life or the lives of other people by preventing an accident.

Smart Or Dumb – Does It Matter?

No discussion on training would be complete without referring to theories on the intelligence of dogs. Hundreds of books are dedicated to the subject. Some say the smarter the dog, the harder it is to train; the less clever, the easier. But, smart or dumb, does it matter? Isn't it more important how well-behaved our dogs are?

I have reservations about using the word 'intelligence' in relation to dogs because it's not only too simplistic, it's also unfair. Although Dr Stanley Coren has developed an interesting and enjoyable intelligence test that you can try on your dog, IQ tests are no basis for predicting future success in training.

Many people also make the incorrect assumption that intelligence varies according to breed. There have even been IQ tests done on dogs to determine the cleverest breeds, and I hope that Dr Coren will forgive me for rejecting the table he gives in his book *The Intelligence of Dogs*. I think it's nonsense, but if you're curious, I'll tell you that the dogs at the top of the table are breeds like standard poodles and German shepherds. The one with the lowest IQ is – I hate to bow to cliché – long-legged, beautiful, with long blond hair: the lovely Afghan.

One of the main reasons why so many people believe that Labradors and border collies are cleverer, because better behaved, than all others is because of the mentality of their owners. There is no doubt that many owners of German shepherds, for instance, have better-behaved dogs than the owners of bichons or King Charles spaniels. Many owners of medium-sized and big dogs are, both by necessity and choice, more accepting of muddy boots and ready to throw a tennis ball to keep up with their active dogs. Also, it's easier socially to get away with a pint-sized dog acting badly than a larger one, whose greater size magnifies its naughtiness. Small dogs can always be picked up if they are trying to bite the postman. This isn't so easily done with a Rottweiler.

But the question still remains: what is the nature of canine intelligence. IQ tests don't take into consideration the two basic types of dog intelligence: intelligence based on instinct and intelligence based on the ability to adapt to a changing set of circumstances.

Instinctive intelligence and adaptive intelligence

Instinctive intelligence comprises the behaviours and skills provided by genetics. This is the form of intelligence that gives herding dogs the basic skills to herd and retrievers to retrieve. Therefore a dog's breed is generally a very good indicator of his instinctive intelligence. Different breeds are better at different tasks. Border collies, for instance, are brilliant at herding but their natural fox-hunting abilities are practically non-existent. A basset hound can't be bothered to herd but has the sharpest nose in the business, making him a superior tracker. There is no single task or ability that gives one breed an edge over another in overall intelligence. So it can't be said that one breed is cleverer than another. It's like comparing apples and oranges. Furthermore, shame on us for judging their intelligence by the way they obey us.

In addition, instinctive intelligence is what gives dogs some of their most special qualities, like their nurturing side. Probably everyone has known or heard of a dog that, when anyone in his family is ill, takes up vigil on that person's bed. Wolves do this in the wild as well, sitting by an injured or sick member of their pack, trying to keep him warm, often bringing food to him until he dies or recovers. This is partly a result of being a member of the canine social pack, but mostly it is one of those genetic mechanisms that many animals have; it's called the species preservation mechanism.

By contrast with instinctive intelligence, adaptive intelligence is entirely individual. As we'll see later in this chapter, it consists of three elements: learning ability, memory ability and problem-solving ability.

Your Dog's Trainability

I believe that what's more important than intelligence is an individual dog's capacity for learning and improving, in combination, of course, with your dedication and ability. In a clinical study I did several years ago I compared the physical build of individual dogs across a broad spectrum of breeds with temperament and ability to learn. I'll spare you the technical details, but I concluded that there was a strong correlation among these factors. The optimal level of training was achieved with dogs that displayed a calm temperament and had a strong build. If you're looking for the easiest dog to train, you should consider a strongly built dog with a tranquil manner.

A dog's nervous disposition also plays a part in his trainability. My view is that there are four main characteristics of their nervous system, and these give us what we call a choleric, phlegmatic, sanguine or melancholic dog. We can look at these characteristics by way of other indicators: first, the strength of the nervous system; second, excitability and inhibition and their balance within the nervous system; and third, mobility, or speed, of nervous reactions.

A choleric dog is one who has a strong nervous disposition, lacks temperamental balance and can quickly regulate his emotions.

A dog with a phlegmatic nervous system is one who has a strong nervous disposition, is fairly balanced and calm, but can only regulate his emotions slowly.

A sanguine dog has a strong nervous system, is fairly balanced, and is able to regulate his emotions quickly.

Finally, a melancholic dog has a weak nervous disposition, lacks balance and can either be very slow or very fast in regulating his emotions He is temperamentally very unstable, susceptible to veering between extreme highs and lows with great speed.

The best nervous disposition for training is the sanguine. This type of dog is highly efficient, well balanced, reliable, precise, confident, and can be used in roles ranging from pet to guard dog.

If you're working with dogs and therefore must select the right dog for a particular job, you'll certainly have to choose carefully one suitable for that function. But when we're talking about our beloved pets, we're stuck with the nervous system that they have come with, as well as their learning and behavioural ability. Although some qualities are flexible – you may influence or interchange the reactions a dog displays to one or another stimulus – on the whole you have to work with what you've got.

To be a good handler you have to develop the skills to communicate with dogs of all temperaments and nervous inclinations. I'm not only going to show you the basics of training your dog to do nearly anything a dog can do, but I'll teach you how to be flexible in training your dog, whatever his disposition.

Coffee, a Weimaraner, aged one.

Classical conditioning

There are two basic ways by which dogs learn: classical conditioning and operant conditioning. Classical conditioning theory, which was developed by Ivan P. Pavlov, refers to the way animals associate things. When a dog hears the doorbell, he knows someone's at the door. When he hears his food being put in his bowl, he knows it's time to eat. How does he know this? Well, when something happens more than once in similar circumstances, he begins to associate one event (the doorbell ringing) leading to another (visitors coming in). This form of conditioning means that, after a few repetitions, a dog doesn't need a primary reinforcer, like food, to get excited about something such as the sight of his feeding bowl (a secondary reinforcer).

Classical conditioning is the greatest tool we will be teaching you to use as it will enable you to cover a variety of subjects from coping with a dog that has a soft mouth, to teaching your dog to be tolerant of fireworks and thunder, to love the postman and to be dog- or any other creature-friendly. Sexual responses, fear responses and waste elimination can all be classically conditioned.

Operant conditioning

Operant conditioning refers to the way animals learn that their behaviour has consequences. In this manner of obtaining information, a dog realises that the results of his actions depend exclusively on himself. Every action leads to a certain reaction – the principle of cause and effect. You sit – you get a goody. You don't sit – nothing happens. According to renowned American educational psychologist Edward Lee Thorndike, this is the Law of Effect in action: if a consequence is pleasant, the preceding behaviour becomes more likely. If a consequence is unpleasant, the preceding behaviour becomes less likely.

In her book *Excel-Erated Learning* Pamela Reid describes the four scenarios of operant conditioning and their effectiveness in training. In summary, these are:

Positive reinforcement. You present something good, like a treat or a toy, as a result of a desired behaviour. Such behaviour is more likely to occur again in the future.

Negative reinforcement. You take away a bad consequence when a desired behaviour has occurred. For instance, your dog agrees to lie down so that you'll take your foot off his short lead. Or he stops pulling on his lead to keep you from cutting short his walk by turning round and going home. As in the first scenario, this increases the likelihood of the desired behaviour recurring.

Positive punishment. A bad consequence is delivered when an undesired behaviour occurs. This is what we normally think of first when we think of punishment. A negative behaviour receives a negative consequence. Your dog pulls on the lead; you check him with it. Unlike the two previous scenarios, this decreases the likelihood of the desired behaviour occurring in the future.

Negative punishment. A positive reward is removed when an undesired behaviour occurs. You ask your dog to sit but he lies down, so he doesn't get his ball to play with. You ask your dog to come to you so you can put his lead on for a walk, but he doesn't come and instead races around the house in excitement, so he misses out on his walk.

Like positive punishment, this method of conditioning decreases the possibilities of the desired behaviour recurring.

Now let's look in more detail at those three aspects of adaptive intelligence that I mentioned earlier: learning ability, memory ability and problem-solving ability.

Learning ability
There are five basic ways in which dogs employ their learning ability, and they learn with varying degrees of competence and speed.

Observational learning. This is the natural, incidental learning that allows your dog to form associations between conditions and outcomes by solely observing them. A good example is when your dog tries to catch a ball simply because other dogs are doing it. Or maybe you've seen him trying to open the fridge door just after watching you do so.

Monty (left) and buddies Bella and Bijou.

I have a canine friend called Bijou, a border collie, who loves to watch TV because she enjoys seeing the animals on the screen. She's a big fan of the *National Geographic* and *Discovery* channels. As soon as her owner clicks on the remote, no matter where Bijou is in the house, she comes running. The click is her signal to run to the TV room, and, of course, watching TV is the reward. In the past she has even tried to work the remote, albeit unsuccessfully. (Bijou's owners also put the TV on when they leave the house. Whether she watches much then is in question; she probably just naps, but the TV most likely soothes her as it's something pleasing and familiar. Certainly it makes the owners feel less guilty when they have to leave Bijou behind for a short time.)

Environmental learning. Here a dog learns a mental map of his environment, so that he knows where certain activities occur (eating in the kitchen, playing ball in the garden), where his toys and other common objects are, and where his family members are usually to be found (Mum at her computer, the children in the family room).

Social learning. This involves learning to respond to emotional and social signs, whether human or canine. For instance, a dog learns that when a person is happy they are more likely to be affectionate towards him. On the other hand, when a person is angry it's best to take cover.

This is a good time to admit that my own dogs jump up on me when I come home, although I don't allow them to do this with strangers. I love it and no one can convince me that I should stop them from doing so. They also seem to be able to gauge whether or not I need a big welcome or just to be left alone when I get home. They can read my emotional signals better than my own family can.

And we're all familiar with the dog that snarls at his owners or anyone else coming near while he's chewing on a bone. The dog gets what he wants: to be left alone. Snarl = Bone + Peace. But what's the message here for us? We're wrong to allow such behaviour and need to address the problem urgently before someone is injured.

One of the most extraordinary facts of our life is that, although we are besieged at every moment by impressions from our sensory surface, we notice so very small a part of them... Yet the physical impressions which do not count are there as those which do, and affect our sense organs just as energetically. Why they fail to pierce the mind is a mystery.
William James, Attention, 1892

Language comprehension. This refers to a dog's ability to learn human verbal signals. With proper training, dogs can learn the meaning of words. Not in the sense that they can understand syntax or grammar, but in the sense that they can understand what's expected of them when they hear a certain command. They quickly form verbal associations with or without our help and pick up the meaning of certain words, phrases and even sentences.

Within their physical limits, dogs can be trained to understand and follow a multitude of commands. The following anecdote is for illustrative purposes only; don't try this at home!

There is an episode in the TV detective series *Columbo* called 'How to Dial a Murder'. A murderer successfully trains his two Dobermanns, named after famous movie characters, to kill his wife's lover. He trains them using a combination of signals: a ringing telephone and the word 'Rosebud' (he was a serious film buff, not to mention mad as a hatter). Thankfully, the dogs are eventually 'reprogrammed' and trained to kiss people at the sound of the same signals instead of killing them (although this occurs after the said lover meets a grisly demise at the jaws of the dogs before they are retrained). Only Columbo's humanity and exceptional sleuthing talents saves the dogs from being destroyed.

This is a far-fetched example, to be sure, but it certainly brings home the point that dogs can be trained to understand human words and signals. Of course, *you* will only be training your dog to do positive and responsible things. They aren't yours to make into sinister creatures for your own dark purposes!

Many canine behaviourists and trainers have attempted to calculate the amount of verbal signals dogs can actually comprehend. Estimates run from as few as 50 to as many as 270. But such tests are flawed, as signals that are understood by one dog may be entirely different from those understood by another. Also, human error may be to blame: a dog that has been tested and knows only 50 signals with one person may learn double or even triple that number with another. I personally believe the sky's the limit when it comes to dogs' potential to understand us.

Task learning. Here a dog's active involvement is required. He can learn a task like 'fetch' on a trial-and-error basis, eventually achieving the result you wish through specific signals and rewards. If you command your dog to 'stay' and he gets a treat every time he does so (but at no other time – for instance when he half-heartedly stays), he'll eventually understand that you expect him to stay where he is every time you say the word.

This is the particular type of learning that show-biz dogs in particular have to master. Eddie, the tenacious canine star of the hit TV series *Frasier* is a wonderful example of how a dog can employ his task-learning abilities, and, in my view, he's the best-trained dog ever to appear on television. From rolling over 'dead' in disgust at his human companions, to putting his hands over his face in embarrassment, or presenting his lead for his walk, Eddie does his all stunts on cue. The little fellow's timing is so perfect, and he's always facing the right way, that he gives us the impression that he is simply following his script and doing it beautifully. And it's all because he gets persistent and consistent commands from his skilful trainer.

Memory ability

Just as we humans differ in our short- and long-term abilities where memory is concerned, so do dogs. Short-term memory is just that, a memory that only lasts a very short time, like if you get a phone number from directory enquiries and dial it straight away. Most of us will forget the number and not be able to recite it minutes later. A long-term memory is nearly a permanent one, and this is the one we want to stimulate and condition when we're training our dogs to heed our commands.

Animals, like men, attend now to one thing, now to another. There are two aspects of the problem. Of the stimuli impinging on peripheral receptors only a few are effective at any one time in determining the animal's response. Secondly, it seems certain that only some features of the stimuli present at any one time are actually stored in memory.
Karl Lashley

FREDDY

Much to his owners' annoyance and everyone else's, Freddy, a chow chow I had in training, loves to chase cats (among other things). And everywhere Freddy has ever spied a cat when out on his walkies, he dives towards that place, pulling his master along with him – or running for miles when allowed off the lead. Behind an iron gate, under a bush, Freddy recalls every cat's hiding place and shivers in anticipation as he nears each spot. He lives in an adrenalin-charged state at the prospect of finding a cat where once he had seen one before. Luckily, training can work wonders on problems like this, as we will see later on.

Freddy demonstrates how powerful a dog's long-term memory is. But it was a very unhelpful memory for his owner, who was constantly in physiotherapy for a sore shoulder. But that's not the worst of it. I'm told that Freddy has run up vet's bills exceeding £20,000 as he has had to have two titanium plates inserted into his legs after surviving two road accidents.

People often tell me that their dog is great in training classes but when they are out on their own with him, he fails to cooperate. It isn't that the dog isn't trying to cooperate and wants to punish his owner. It's primarily that his memory is too good and he is confused by the imprecise signals that we humans are apt to give. If you teach your dog to come to you across a hall or even to pass other dogs in class, that is what he'll learn and that's what he'll do.

Also, look where your hands are during training. Examine your confidence, the tone of your voice, your distance from the dog and your body language. Even the time of day or your clothing can be responsible for your dog's seemingly inconsistent responses. Have you remembered to bring along treats and are you handing them out at the same intervals as when you were in a training class? Every element is important in making your command successful. Dogs remember exactly what you did in issuing it and exactly what *they* did that won them their reward. It's up to you to keep replicating your command exactly the same way, as clearly as you can, especially in the early stages of training.

Problem-solving ability

Problem solving is perhaps the most important of a dog's learning abilities. It's his ability to find solutions to problems (commands from his owner) that allow him to overcome obstacles to win himself a reward (treat, toy, pat on the back). Problem solving incorporates planning and choosing behaviours that lead to a solution, the capacity to remember other skills or knowledge from past problem-solving situations, and the successful transfer of these to the present problem. Dogs with a strong, confident and balanced nervous disposition will do far better at these tests. They will use their entire repertoire of skills and not give up until they've cracked the problem.

Consider the elements of agility training. When dogs are first learning how to go through this exciting obstacle course, they have to figure out what to do to win their reward. The tunnel is a perfect example here. How do you get the dog to go through this long, narrow object and appear at the other end? The commonest way of doing it requires two people, one holding the dog at one end and another squatting on the other end, looking back through the tube and holding a treat. Normally the dog has two choices: go through the tube to get to the treat or go around the outside of the tube to get the treat. But if he does the latter, he won't get the treat. Some dogs will have a harder time solving this puzzle. If they don't grasp it, a treat can be placed in the middle of the tube and the dog can be coaxed to the far end to win another.

After a bit of trial and error he'll figure out he has to go through the tube to get the treat. Only a true professional will be able to work with and motivate a dog that tries to get away from the whole scenario or sinks his teeth into someone to show his displeasure. Well, we all try to solve things in our own way!

A great way to start building your dog's problem-solving abilities is, of course, to give him problems to solve. Take it slowly, repeating exercises several times until you feel he has mastered them. Hand Feeding challenges are the simplest brainteasers your dog will face, but there are many more. Some are real party tricks. For instance, stand with something small in one closed hand and hold out in front of you both this fist and the other hand, also closed but with nothing in it. When he looks, paws or sniffs at the hand that holds the treat, reward him with it. Do this a few times. Your dog will find this simple as all he's doing is following his nose, and, of course, he saw which hand the treat went into anyway.

Now make it a little harder. Forget the treat. Put one hand out in a fist and the other hand out flat, palm up. Only reward the dog when he goes for the open hand. To start with, he only has to look briefly at it to win a reward. But then get a little more demanding and wait for him to touch his nose to your palm or swat it with his paw. Reward him every time he does what you want.

At the Good Boy Dog School we often play games with young

pups that involve empty yogurt pots with a little dried dog food in them, standing up or capsized. Tins with treats in them, Kong toys and hollow bones keep puppies entertained for hours. These games have the added, crucial benefit of teaching your dog to use his brain and rely on himself to solve problems instead of looking to you or giving up to go and destroy the back garden instead.

Dogs are born with great potential, but it is up to us to help them develop their abilities and achieve the intelligence that they are capable of forming. Sadly, most dogs never reach their true potential. In fact, the majority barely scratch the surface of all that they are capable of accomplishing.

There are many kinds of problem-solving games you can play with your dog that will help him to improve his learning abilities and at the same time have a lot of fun. These games appear throughout Chapter 4, as part of our Hand Feeding method.

Jake and Meg.

Chapter 3
Preparing for Training

I used to look at [my dog] Smokey and think 'If you were a little smarter you could tell me what you were thinking,' and he'd look at me like he was saying 'If you were a little smarter, I wouldn't have to.'
Fred Jungclaus

Above all, my training method is about enjoying your dog and he you. My training method isn't about dominance. Instead, this five-step programme (which we explain in detail in Chapters 4–8) is about ensuring success in training and keeping your dog happy. It is about knowing what you want and what your dog should do, and then employing this knowledge in a variety of circumstances so that eventually he'll act of his own free will.

Now that you've joined our school, it's a very lucky dog that has you as his owner. I bet you can't wait to take him out on his initial training exercise. You're nearly ready.

Tools of the Trade

First, as part of learning how to be the best possible teacher for your dog, you'll need to equip yourself with the right training gear. Back in the Ukraine, one of my first teachers and lecturers at the Kennel Club's instructor-training courses, Sokolinskiy Leonid, for whom I had the greatest respect, asked our class at the start what we felt we needed to begin training. Various answers followed, including treats, lead, collar, free time, space, and so on. One smart student even said a dog. They were all correct, but the response Leonid was really looking for was a pen and paper, so that we could write detailed notes on how we were going to go about the process of dog training: regimes and routines, schedules, frequency of lessons and a brief summary of what we wanted to achieve. You may not be interested in becoming a professional dog trainer, but the lesson everyone who wants to learn dog training should draw from Leonid is that *you need to be prepared*.

The following list sets out everything you'll need from the start, and will put you in good stead to begin training your dog.

Positive stimulation and rewards

• Your dog's food, titbits or any sort of edible and delicious doggie treats, carried accessibly in a pouch, bag or pocket.

• A ball for playing together, and maybe a couple of other favourite toys. (For more on positive stimulation, see Teaching Techniques, p. 49.)

Equipment

In my opinion, it's not what you use, but how you use it. In this vein, it's much better to watch a professional handler using training tools than to read about how they are used. These are the basic items you'll need:

• A durable, soft collar of nylon or canvas, the right width for your dog and correctly adjusted (it should always be tight enough not to pass over the dog's head but loose enough for you to be able to slip at least two fingers under it). At my school we don't approve of choke chains and similar restraining devices. We don't recommend harnesses either, but use one if you prefer. Bear in mind that leather, while looking good, requires a lot of care, isn't that durable and can easily snap when wet or punctured with extra holes.

Willy

• Dog tag. This sounds obvious, but many people forget to put one on their dog. An identity tag is required by law. On every dog I work with, I put my own tag, along with the owner's, for extra security.

• A short lead, 3–3.5 feet long, and a long line of 10 feet or more. I personally carry a 30-foot lunging rein in my training bag as it gives enough free run but also allows me to keep the dog under proper control at all times.

• A negative marker (for instance, training discs) for some parts of your training. We discuss the use of these in Corrections (p.129), but, depending on your dog's behaviour, you may not require them.

• Bundles of poop bags. Responsible owners pick up after their dogs at all times.

• A comfortable rug or blanket to crash on, as neither you nor your dog may last long at the start. This is also useful when training in cold or wet weather; sitting or lying on wet or frozen ground can be unpleasant for many dogs.

• Access to plenty of water. Training is thirsty work for dogs, as the treats and the exercise both make them dry. Water isn't so important during short walks or brief training intervals, but for longer sessions, especially in warm weather, it's vital.

• A first-aid kit. It's best to have one at home and/or in the car, so that you feel prepared for any emergency. Also, it's important to know how to use it. It's never too late to learn and it might just come in handy.

• Emergency information. You should keep your vet's daytime and 24-hour numbers handy, as well as your dog's insurance details. It's also wise to let a close friend or relative know when you're going out so that they can come to your rescue if need be.

• A clicker. This is an optional training tool but one I highly recommend. Clicker training was developed by the American dog trainer Karen Pryor and has revolutionised dog training. I value it as an additional training tool as it uses precise, positive reinforcement. (The clicker is discussed in more detail in Hand Feeding, p. 71.)

All this, you say? I'll need a backpack just to take my dog for a walk! You won't, in fact, though at first it is a lot of equipment to coordinate, but you'll get the hang of it soon enough. Excess leads can be strapped to your belt and treats can be placed in a pouch that can also hang from your waist in a bum bag or from a belt loop.

Don't be afraid to be creative. You can easily identify my clients as most of them look like cowboys wearing holsters! The trick is to keep your hands free as much as possible to give hand signals and deliver rewards or another form of stimulus at the proper times. Keep everything at hand around your waist and in easily accessible pockets. My favourite denim waistcoat, which I've been using for the past ten years for training, has 16 pockets. It makes me look like a hippie, but the dogs are glued to it and it keeps me organised.

Whatever behaviour you're trying to establish in your dog, it won't take you very long. Don't let all this preparation work frighten you. Soon you'll be able to enjoy your walks, watch the sunset and admire the landscape with your pet. This will be the reward for all your hard work.

How To Be a Good Teacher

The theories we discussed in Chapter 2 are very useful for understanding how dogs think. But, as teachers to our dogs, we also need practical methods that help us to train them in the most effective way. Pamela Reid describes four stages of learning through which a dog progresses during training.

Stage 1: Acquisition. This is the gaining of new information by the dog. When we're teaching a new command, the dog must figure out – with our guidance – what he is being asked to do and how to accomplish it.

Stage 2: Fluency. Trainers use this term to refer to the dog's natural, automatic reaction to the information. When a dog has understood what is expected on being requested to do a certain task and doesn't hesitate to produce a correct response, he has become 'fluent' at it. As trainers, we can work on the speed and accuracy of his reactions.

Stage 3: Generalisation. When a dog learns that the information he has learned can be applied to other situations, he has learned to generalise.

Stage 4: Maintenance practice. Once a dog has accomplished the first three stages, he'll need to practise, otherwise the speed and proficiency of his responses to your commands will weaken. Even when the practice period is over, it is still very useful to take your dog for a short refresher course every now and then.

Training is all about having fun.

Now we know how our dogs put things together, we can concentrate on how we can become good teachers to our canine pals. Above all, good training requires you to both *inform* and *motivate* your dog. You must assume that he doesn't know what's right from wrong until you inform him. And you can't expect him to do as you wish and to want to do what you wish unless you motivate him. Information and motivation are a powerful combination. If, every time the doorbell rings, the new arrival has a treat in their hand, the dog that sits down will learn that nice things happen when visitors come.

Now let's consider what you must do to be a good teacher.

Use your dog's name. It is important to 'condition-use' your dog's name to the required task. There is no point in trying to come up with some other name or nickname if he's never heard it before in training. Instead of using a variety of names, you're better off not using one at all – just the command.

Also, it is important, when you wish your dog to do something, to call him by his name and then follow up with a command or suitable gesture. Sounds obvious, doesn't it? But, without knowing it, many of us call our dog by name without asking him to do anything and we get frustrated when he can't figure out what we want even if he is happy to please. Dogs can't read our minds – well, not all the time anyway! So do them a favour and ask them properly what you'd like them to do.

Of course, later you may wish to broaden the range of names you use for your dog as the repertoire of commands you give him expands. He'll learn these as further building blocks of his vocabulary. But, in the beginning, keep it simple. In this way you'll be helping your dog to pick up a suitable reflex rather than constantly being stuck with the puzzle of your instructions and, in response, simply learning to ignore them.

Be consistent in your commands and signals. Don't make up different words and different signals for the same thing. At least to begin with, stick to one word and one signal. It doesn't matter what they are as long as you can remember them and always use them. It is also helpful to duplicate the same tone when speaking a command. Your dog will learn that when you keep it short, like 'Sit', he'd better do it right away, whereas 'William, darling, will you please sit for Mummy?' will probably have no impact at all.

Be consistent in giving rewards. Especially in the early stages, you'll need to give your dog a reward for every correct response he gives and sometimes just for half a response or an intention to do it. Only later, when he has a firm comprehension of your commands, can you begin to give treats less often. Still, some sort of reward will always benefit you both – for instance, praising or releasing him, or giving a sign of approval such as a reassuring stroke.

Be proactive, not reactive. The more organised and knowledgeable you are about the behaviour of dogs, the problems that arise and the solutions available to you, the better prepared you'll be to tackle issues before they present difficulties. Dogs change over time, especially in their early years when they are growing. Males come into their own, for instance, and often exhibit domineering qualities. But, if you're aware of the potential problems and how you can deal with them, you'll be better equipped to act before you see the first signs.

The key is to prevent bad habits from forming by getting on top of them early. Being ahead of the game allows you to form the right response in your dog, to establish a good habit. It is much harder to have to condition a dog out of a bad habit than to stop it from happening in the first place, before it can become a learned behaviour.

Watch your body language. When you're asking your dog to do something, make sure that your body language makes sense in terms of what you want him to do. For instance, when first teaching your dog to do a sit-stay, don't go and play with another dog. Wait until later, when you and your dog are ready to use this as a method of distraction to improve his response. In fact, eventually you'll want your dog to be able to function without hand signals, as he won't always be facing you.

Be persistent in your training. We mentioned this earlier, but it's crucial enough to repeat: it's not good enough to ask your dog to do something one day and mean it, and another day not mean it. You'll only confuse him about the importance of obeying you. And, at all times, you must be ready to deliver a reward or other stimulus when you deliver a command. Otherwise, don't ask!

Be precise in your timing. Immediately after your dog responds in some way to your command, you must be ready to deliver an appropriate stimulus that will educate him about the best way to carry out the command in the future. It's no good following up minutes later: he won't know for what he is being rewarded or corrected. Your reaction must be as closely timed with his response as possible. You'll probably achieve a 99% success rate if you react in the first couple of seconds after he responds; 50–60% if you acknowledge his actions after three to five seconds; and somewhere between 0–20% if you react ten seconds afterwards.

Command with confidence. Just as we don't respect a weak boss, so we must not appear weak or unconfident to our dogs. A strong voice is always helpful, but it doesn't have to be loud to be commanding. Your dog won't learn anything better just because you're saying it louder.

In the beginning a confident tone will help your dog understand you best. But, overall, it isn't what and how you deliver your command that is most important, but what your command means. Once a command is properly conditioned and learned, your dog will probably be able to understand what you mean whether you whisper it or shout it. Whispering, as long as the stimulus remains the same, will produce the same conditioning as any other tone of voice.

Never give up! Sometimes we get frustrated because our dog either doesn't understand what we're asking him to do or doesn't *want* to do it. Just as a school teacher can't give up on difficult pupils – otherwise he's a bad teacher – so we can't give up on our dogs. We need to search out creative solutions. Training dogs is about *teaching*; it's a challenge you need to take on with gusto and determination.

If you have a boisterous and unsettled dog, you won't want to wait the five to six years it may take for him to mellow before you start training. Instead, you'll want to harness his energy and direct it in a positive direction. I believe it is possible to work successfully with any dog, but if you aren't succeeding, you must look for outside help. And if you aren't satisfied, get a second opinion or even a third. Eventually you'll find someone who understands you and your dog and can help you.

Be kind at all times. Never lose your temper; there is hardly ever a reason for force. Making your dog do something isn't at all the same as helping and guiding him. Physical punishment is no way to teach man's best friend, your friend. Sadly, training by fear is a method many use, but it is cruel, abusive and not conducive to a happy relationship between you and your dog. Those who engage in such methods aren't worthy of the companionship of dogs.

To be fair, an occasional smack born out of desperation may achieve some results, but you should never allow it to become a way of training. Only an expert in this field can show you properly how to apply the stick-and-carrot approach, and even then, it must be used in a very limited and specific way that can't cause harm. Corrections and reprimands are discussed later (see pp. 129 and 142).

Make training fun. If it's all work, work, work, where's the pleasure, and where is the motivation for either you or your dog? Training is about building a positive relationship between the two of you. Doing endless drills will bore you and him to distraction, and won't endear you to him. Break up your training with games and add them to your training. At my Sunnyhill Park classes we play spoon-and-tennis-ball relay races, wheelbarrow races and musical chairs, to name just a few of the games we use in training. All of these allow us to use our dog-handling skills while having some fun.

On some of my home visits I show my clients how they can sit on the floor and work on static and slow moves while they're watching TV. Training isn't all about rigid sessions but about enjoying the process.

Teaching Techniques

If only training were as easy as giving our dogs a book to read!

There are five main methods by which dogs, and in fact all animals, learn (humans have a sixth, abstract learning). Positive stimulation, negative stimulation, combined stimulation, copying and reinforcement all help, in different ways, to establish communication between you and your dog. When you're able to communicate effectively with him, he can trust you and look to you for guidance.

All the big names in training are expert in administering a combination of the five methods, and with a little practice so will you.

Positive stimulation

As we mentioned in Tools of the Trade (p. 40), you'll need plenty of positive rewards to motivate your dog. These include anything that gets your dog really excited and happy – things that really grab his attention. Perhaps he loves the tug-of-war rope? Or is he barmy about balls? Crazy about cheese? Does he drool deliriously over liver treats? When you want to encourage or reward your dog, give him something that will really make him want to follow your lead. I've found the better the reward, the better the result, especially in the beginning of training. You may have to do a little sleuthing to discover what really lights his fire, but once you've found it, use it!

You won't want to use something that requires a lot of effort or expense, or excites your dog past the point of acceptable behaviour. In time you'll be able to reduce the excitement factor in his reward, when you're sure that his response to your requests won't falter because of it. Also, you'll work out which toys or what kind of play pleases your dog and he feels it is worth working for.

When giving treats as a reward, you won't want to use a smelly, sticky or unhealthy junk food that will harm your dog's health or spoil his appetite by leaving him too full to eat his usual meals. For this reason I recommend you use healthy treats and then gradually switch to his normal diet biscuits and food, maybe with just a little bit of flavour added so that you feel better about cutting out the treats.

Eventually your dog will want to work hard for your approval and he'll be happy with any little thing you give him. In time you too will find that you won't need to reward him for every good thing he does, only after a successful routine or at the end of a good walk.

Using positive stimulation has the added and important benefit of demonstrating to your dog that *you* are *the* best source of good things in life. And even when he doesn't find you to be his most exciting option, at least your rewards will be a guaranteed and safe choice. If you're able to achieve this, you'll have no trouble calling your dog away from other dogs, picnics, joggers, games of football and other sporting activities, because he'll see you and your smorgasbord of rewards as the best things on offer.

Negative stimulation

Unfortunately, this is often seen as one of the key elements of dog training. We've been bombarded over the years with the misguided recommendation of choke chains and yanking leads. Ask most people what they need to train a dog and you'll get a dreadful list full of things like rolled-up newspapers, choke chains and rubbing your dog's nose in his business. It doesn't have to be so. You can train your dog much more agreeably and better without these archaic methods.

Just as a positive stimulus leaves your dog wishing for and trying to work out how to win more, a negative stimulus delivers an unpleasant feeling to him, one which he'll want to remember to avoid in the future. This can be something as mild as taking your eyes off him to tell him he hasn't done something correctly.

Negative stimulation is a very difficult method to master and I don't advise anyone who is new to dog training or who is short-tempered to use it. Although negative stimuli can work very well in good hands, my advice is to read about them later in Corrections (p. 129) and decide whether they are suitable for you, as well as necessary to train your dog. You won't want to use them on a dog that doesn't deserve them.

Combined (or complex) stimulation

This is the use of both positive and negative stimuli, otherwise known as 'stick and carrot'. Used in combination, positive and negative stimuli are a highly effective way to communicate with your dog. Your own preference and your dog's character should together determine the balance of the two kinds of stimulation. However, he'll certainly need many more instances of encouragement than negative stimulation if you are to communicate your meaning effectively. You probably know the game of 'Hot and Cold', where you try to direct someone to an object using just these two words. Well, if you used only 'cold' or only 'hot', it would be much harder in most cases for your team mate to find the hidden object. Use both of the prompts, and your team mate will be able to find it more readily. It can be the same in dog training. You may well need a balance of both positive and negative stimuli to train your dog effectively and with greater ease.

Copying

Dogs learn some things through copying the actions of humans or other dogs. Gardeners who have dogs often see this. The dog watches them dig, and then follows suit. Pure imitation. How I wish it was always this easy! In training, copying can be used to teach your dog, for instance, to jump over hurdles in the agility obstacle course. Dogs often try to run around them, or, if they're small enough, under them. So how do you teach a dog to go *over* them instead? Let him follow you or another dog jumping the hurdles a few times until he makes the connection.

Reinforcement

This is a rather curious, but nevertheless effective, teaching technique. Instead of needing to teach your dog a certain move, you can wait for this to occur naturally and reward him for it, thus reinforcing in him the idea that he has done the right thing. For instance, when your dog lies down on his own without your asking or making him, you can reinforce this action with rewards. Very soon he'll lie down because he wants that reward. This approach can be applied to all sorts of moves that you might want him to make. Simply observe his behaviour, note it and reinforce it when it occurs.

Jake takes a break.

REAL Training

Gary Wilkes, one of my favourite trainers, devised the 'REAL' way to plan a dog-training programme. I've found his advice invaluable in helping trainees to become better handlers:

(R)aise your training standards. Your dog will get bored if he's always asked to do the same things over and over again. Try raising the bar and giving him challenges. You'll also achieve more by asking more. But watch your pace, as it's easy to get ahead of yourself.

(E)xtras for excellence. It's time to reward good behaviour. It makes your dog think positively. But what if he's done something exceptional? Let him feel the full glory of the moment. He won't be able to misinterpret your rewarding him lavishly, and he may want to try his very best for you every time in the future because he knows what good things are in store for him if he does.

(A)nticipate the error. If you're aware of your dog's weaknesses, you can help guide him through the learning process. I understand the dog owner whose dog has just done something terrible for the first time. But I can't understand anyone whose dog repeatedly does the same bad things. As a dog owner you have to figure out what you will allow your dog to do and what you will not, and have a plan to thwart bad behaviour.

I know a Jack Russell that likes to throw herself at people when she's walking off the lead. The owner knows this and when she sees her dog begin to veer off in the direction of a human for a cuddle, she gives the command 'Come!' The moment the dog decides to comply, the owner rewards her, making her completely forget that she wanted to run off full throttle at some unsuspecting, perhaps even anti-dog, person. A dog owner must be prepared and able at all times to eradicate or at least manage a dog's unsociable behaviour.

(L)ots of repetitions. Your dog will only learn if he practises and consistently accomplishes the task at hand with consistent rewards from you. Doing loads of repetitions also prevents him from forgetting what your commands mean. In this way you make sure that all the short-memory files are transferred to the long-term memory, making them automatic responses.

When To Begin Training? Now!

No matter how old your dog is when he scampers through your front door, the ideal time to begin training him is at that very moment. Any later and you're playing catch-up, which is by far the hardest way to train. Of course, some owners decide that it's time to train an adult dog that they've neglected to train during the years they've had him, while others take on adult rescue dogs. Fortunately, it's possible to train these too.

Training puppies

For many years the stereotype for dog training was to let puppies enjoy their puppyhood and start training them when they reached 9–12 months, or even later. In recent times this approach has almost disappeared, and at the Good Boy Dog School we recommend starting to train your pup as early as you receive him, or in the case of a breeder, as early as four weeks of age.

Gem

Pups are born into this world as helpless as human babies. Just ten days after birth, however, a puppy is able to see and hear, its sense of smell is almost complete, it can move about and conquer simple obstacles, as well as solve some problems on its own. In many countries puppies just four weeks old are separated from their lactating mothers and sold on. Their brains at this age are remarkably mature; they respond adequately to outside stimuli, actively learn by trial and error, and are capable of gaining and storing information that they will retain for the rest of their lives.

I don't accept the common belief that a dog year is equivalent to seven human years, or six or five, for that matter, as is often suggested nowadays. I see a one-year-old puppy as the equivalent of a young person of 15–18. Do you send your children to pre-school at that age? Of course not!

A puppy's brain at just four weeks can absorb any skill it can put its paws or teeth into, and it will actively search for cues and clues that will guide it through the rest of its life. Because of this, if you leave a pup to its own devices, it will educate itself. But how many dog owners can tell you that their dogs learned all their good habits all by themselves? It never happens. Some say that they never had to train their last dog and that he was immaculately behaved. They aren't giving themselves enough credit. Whether they know it or not, they trained their dog to cohabit with them successfully without realising it. This is certainly the case sometimes, as not every owner needs formal training. Some people are able to form a natural communication with their dog that works without their having gone to a single dog-training class. But not everyone is lucky enough to have these skills.

If you're still not convinced that good training starts at the earliest possible time, consider the story of how Emily and I sealed the deal to publish this book. We brought along Dexter, a three-month-old Jack Russell, who was fully house-trained, working reliably off the lead and performing an exciting repertoire of over 40 fancy tricks. Amazing, you say? Well then, try our Hand Feeding method. You'll see amazing results with your puppy too.

Our training debunks common training myths as well. The approach we use is kindness and winning over our dogs so that they want to follow our instructions. Hand Feeding is the most comprehensive, easy and logical play-style method and should be introduced to your pup as soon as you get him.

Training adult dogs

An adult dog entering your home, no matter what his origin, will have no idea of your routines, rules and expectations. Therefore his training and instruction should begin the moment he walks through your door – or even a few days before, if possible, so that he gets to know you and your family at the earliest opportunity. Your prepared-ness should begin as soon as you've decided to take on an adult dog.

It is never easy at first, just as it is never simple when a new person moves into your home with their own habits and preferences. Many think it's intelligent to let a dog settle and relax and get used to his surroundings. But in this time he'll be establishing his own routines, irrespective of your wishes. By training your dog from the outset you'll give him far more reason to relax and enjoy himself, as you'll be interacting with him, rewarding him for his compliance and showing him his boundaries, leaving little room for confusion and misbehaviour. His good behaviour will make you happy and relaxed, which will make him happy and relaxed, as well as winning him rewards.

So how do you begin to start to train him when you don't even speak each other's language? Our Hand Feeding method will give you an excellent start and a changed, lifelong outlook. Management solutions (see p. 192) will also give you peace of mind. Establish your rules clearly from day one. Your new family member should learn where you want him to sleep, as well as where, when and how you'll feed and exercise him. You'll also want to show him the good things that happen when he acts according to your needs and wishes. Be sensible and don't have unrealistic expectations of your dog. You'll want to study our tips on managing your dog's chewing and soiling habits, barking and jumping up, possessiveness and attacking (see Chapter 5) – all the 'baggage' that rescue dogs carry with them to some degree.

Before we get started on your training I'll give you one of the most effective methods to establish a rescue dog in your home and begin to rehabilitate him. Attach a short lead to his collar and clip the other end to your belt loop, making the two of you inseparable. Let him follow you around the house as you do your chores, or sit and read the paper while he lies quietly by your feet. He'll have no other choice but to follow you, and he won't have the opportunity to urinate on your living room rug or slip out of the back door to chase foxes. You'll be establishing a pattern of good behaviour that tells him how you wish him to be for the rest of his life.

PART 2
THE GOOD BOY DOG SCHOOL
TRAINING PROGRAMME

Sascha.

Chapter 4
Step 1: Eating Out of the Palm of Your Hand

I want my dog making the decisions I would like it to make.
Joanna Hill, competitive obedience trainer

Get ready to teach your dog by Hand Feeding.
Those doggy bowls won't be used for a while.

You're finally ready to begin training your dog and become a proud member of the Good Boy Dog School. There's been a lot of preparation work, and I thank you for your patience. Now the real pleasure and reward of training your dog can start. But, before we start Step 1, a few words on how to get best maximum benefit from my training method.

Our training programme is a progressive one, to be followed in the order given here. Skipping to the section that deals with the problem you think you're having won't help you if you haven't read about my training techniques and followed them one by one. Think of training your dog as being like walking up a steep staircase with him. After each step in the five-step programme, and indeed after each new experience your dog has, you need to stay where you are and make him comfortable and secure with his newly discovered knowledge. In fact, it's harder than climbing stairs, because if you go too far too fast, you'll have to go back a step, maybe more, and get comfortable, and only then should you proceed once more. Don't expect to be able to leap from the bottom step to the top in one flying jump, Superman-style. You'll only become frustrated with your mistakes and erratic progress, and so will your dog.

Training a dog is also a lot like teaching a child mathematics. First you teach the basics: numbers, and how to count up and down.

Then you can introduce addition and subtraction. After a time the child will be able to move on to multiplication and division, building up their skills only when they become comfortable with what they have learned and are ready to tackle more.

Likewise, in dog training you start with basic attitude and obedience training, no matter what your dog's problems and no matter how many or how few these are, because without the basics you won't be able to educate your dog by gentle persuasion and information. I know I'm going to do better and have a much happier relationship with a dog when I start out with a few biscuits in my pocket to reward progress.

It's a pity that some owners choose to bypass gentle means in order to get fast results. I see it all the time, as with a recent arrival, Wooster. I recount his story here as a good example of owners who don't appreciate that training isn't only about educating or re-educating (in the case of a rescue dog or an older dog that has missed out on learning the basics). It's also about building a happy and trusting relationship between owner and dog. Any other technique for getting a dog to follow your will is simply missing the point of the joys of dog ownership.

Jake.

WOOSTER

Wooster, a handsome bearded collie-cross about four years old, is a rescue dog and lived in Birmingham until recently. His owners brought him to London once every few weeks to train him with me. They acquired him two years ago, and although he is very friendly with people he knows and is amenable to training, he is extremely aggressive towards other dogs, lunging with great hostility. As he's a rescue dog who has had three homes, little is known about his upbringing, so we don't know what has caused this negative behaviour. In truth it doesn't really matter. The important point is that he constantly barked and lunged at every dog that came within 50 feet of him, and this had to be stopped. His intention wasn't just to see them off. Even when muzzled, he still attacked ferociously. Wooster's owners, Chris and Polly, wanted to enjoy their walks with him, but his behaviour was making this impossible.

In the first two 90-minute sessions I had with Wooster my main task wasn't to expose him to other dogs, but to try to communicate to him what we expected of him – to listen, to watch and to do as many nice little things as he wanted. In other words, the aim was to get him to focus on being good and acting positively. Wooster didn't have the opportunity to get much exposure to dogs where he lived, so my task was doubly hard because I had to try to make up for all the inhibition about biting during play that he should have learned in his early socialisation.

We had a hard job keeping Wooster occupied while slowly introducing him to other dogs at play, passers-by and other animals. There were exciting achievements, as well as serious (though safe) failures, but the crucial aim of 'desensitisation' worked well. And at each session we could expect more from him. The only thing that can help a dog like Wooster is patience on the part of his owners – of which Chris and Polly seemed to have had great reserves – and persistence.

After a while Wooster began to understand that sticking to a good routine was more rewarding, and he seemed to be really enjoying himself. We also introduced deterrents to counter his negative wants. Attacking was marked as bad behaviour with training discs or by spraying a little water on him. We also tested a remote-controlled citronella anti-bark collar on him (see p. 196). Soon the number and variety of dogs that Wooster *didn't* lunge for rose, and we praised him with great rewards. We even praised him when he was just hanging about, acting pleasantly.

After a few sessions Wooster was sufficiently calm to do some obedience training and took hardly any notice of the dogs around him. Real progress.

But there was still a long way to go. Wooster required many more sessions. His owners needed lots of support and we had a regular exchange of emails where I was able to give them advice even though I couldn't be there to demonstrate and lend a hand. But, as they lived some 120 miles from London and both worked full-time, it wasn't easy. When they wanted to go on holiday I offered to take Wooster for ten days to give him intensive exposure to other dogs and the thorough training he required.

How do you think he did during his stay with me? To be honest, it could have been better. He left a pair of nasty teeth marks on my arm and once almost wandered off around the lake where my doggie gang were exercising. But he was perfect with all the dogs he encountered during his stay. He diverted his efforts into being pleasing. Something inside of him registered that there is lots of good stuff in life, and, importantly, that some things are just not worth trying.

How reliable was Wooster at this stage? *Almost*. 'Almost' is one of those words that gets dogs hit by cars and destroyed. 'Almost' is like saying, 'Oh, my dog doesn't normally do that!' 'Almost' just isn't good enough – unless your dog has nine lives, like a cat.

Unfortunately, I wasn't able to rehabilitate Wooster completely in the ten days I was given. I didn't expect to be able to *cure* him so quickly, but I hoped that I would be able to get him to a level where his owners could manage and work with him further. When I gave him back to his family he still required his muzzle, but his behaviour had been modified greatly.

I've always believed that recent events stay in a dog's mind for some time. They just don't go in one ear and out the other. But what do you do to transfer them into his long-term memory? You recall the knowledge and repeat the experience over and over again, until the dog records it as something vital and worth having stored. Wooster's good behaviour lasted three days after he got home but slowly began to deteriorate to the point where it gave Chris and Polly no pleasure to take him out walking.

Sadly, after a few weeks, they decided to give him up. The commitment required was too much for this working couple. There was also another important factor behind their decision – they were expecting a baby. I volunteered to try to re-home Wooster and in just nine days a new family was recommended by the RSPCA centre I approached. The staff there do a great job of being very selective about who they give their rescue dogs to, by trying to match all the criteria for successful companionship.

The family who rescued Wooster had successfully rehabilitated an aggressive dog in the past, so they knew what they were taking on. I just loved it when the new owner said that she was amazed to find such a perfect dog to smooth over their recent loss.

Five steps to success

This chapter and Chapters 5–8 teach you the five steps of our training programme. The first two chapters are divided into ten sessions of manageable duration. Follow the sessions in the order they appear, but repeat each session until you have achieved a consistent, automatic reaction from your dog and you're fluent at what is required of you. I should tell you here that, even when you have succeeded, you'll need to continue what we call maintenance, to ensure that your dog doesn't slip back into bad habits.

And finally, before you start, I must stress that you'll need to rethink your routine as you progress, as unless you're mentally sharp, organised and precise about this, you'll be less successful than you could be otherwise. Being able to educate your dog involves having to re-educate yourself so that you're always ahead of him, prepared to deal with any expected, and sometimes unexpected, behaviour.

With the first lesson, you will be well on your way to training your dog in the most desirable, enjoyable and effective way. I am confident that you will quickly learn how to communicate with him. The fun has just begun as you and he sharpen your communication skills, continue to learn from each other and advance way beyond your initial hopes.

STEP 1:
EATING OUT OF THE PALM OF YOUR HAND

Your dog is supposed to be ready when you are and do as you ask, but is this the case? Does he look up to you as if to say, 'What's next, Mum [or Dad]?' The problem I often see in my class is not that their dogs aren't trained but that they don't want to be trained. This is a matter of attitude, and our dogs need to have a good one – what we playfully call 'doga-tude' – to train successfully.

Developing a good attitude in your dog is all down to you. It's about you learning how to motivate your dog to want to train with you, and to act willingly as your partner in the process.

The right training spirit

It will be fruitless to try to train your dog if he doesn't have the proper attitude towards learning. If he isn't looking forward to learning anything, you might as well not bother trying to teach him anything until he does. Like a child distracted at school, he won't learn if he's not open to the idea of it. You must get him to understand the concept of asking you for his reward instead of just accepting it as his due. He needs to offer his skills and not just wait to be told what to do. Once your dog is happy to trade his behaviour for your rewards, then he's ready for training. He has the right training spirit – doga-tude!

Often during my outdoor one-to-one training I bring a few dogs with me to act as a distraction for the trainee. This helps to create a natural feel of being in an everyday environment. Also, I always try to train in a busy park or an open space. Often these dogs assist me by acting as demonstration models, serving to illustrate what I'm teaching my student dog. I wish I could teach them everything this way – just by having them watch me and the other dogs!

If I ask one of my 'models' to do something they have never done before, their reaction is to start going through their repertoire of moves, modifying them to try to come up with the positioning or act that I'm asking for. They are keen to figure it out and to be successful.

Puppy Harvey, watching attentively for her next instruction. She has the right training spirit.

But if I were to ask the same thing of my new student dog? The reaction would be quite different. He wouldn't know what I was asking of him, although he may be curious. He may try to figure out what I'm asking for, but most likely he just won't want to know. Typically, he'll go off and sniff or chase something, eager to avoid the situation altogether. However, some new dogs are keener than others. It will take me less time to train a motivated dog than one that isn't, for with the second the owners and I will have to start right from the beginning to alter the dog's attitude. It is far easier to teach a dog that is open-minded and easy-going. You can conquer any behavioural or training problem if you have a dog such as this. Luckily, even if your dog isn't keen now, with my approach he soon will be.

Take a look at Jake's story. He and his owner are a great example of how building a proper attitude to training can overcome just about anything, even physical handicap.

JAKE

Jake is a tri-coloured Tibetan terrier nearly ten months old. He has been deaf from birth. His owner was distraught when she discovered her beautiful puppy couldn't hear her, but the thought of sending him back to the breeder was one she couldn't act on. She loved him too much. Where others may have given up, she was willing to go the extra mile – to persist – and has been rewarded ten times over for her dedication. Jake was lucky he fell into such good hands.

His owner became increasingly concerned about how she'd be able to manage him and his impairment. It became apparent that she was going to need to be able to communicate with him in order to keep him safe and for them to be able to enjoy each other's company.

With a little creativity and time on her part, as well as help from technology, Jake can now do everything non-deaf dogs can do and can respond to signals just like them. The only difference is that his owner can't use voice commands to get his attention to give him instructions. Instead, she must rely on hand signals and a little device, a vibrating collar, that lets Jake know when to look up for cues from her. This handy device hangs around his neck, just like an ordinary collar, and is powered by remote control. Jake's owner pushes a button any time she wants to get his attention to give him a command by hand signal.

But, deaf or not, Jake would not be able to respond to his owner's requests without having gone through our Hand Feeding programme in order to become food-dependent, or rather owner-dependent with the initial help of food. Jake's case is a perfect example of how technology can be used to supplement proper training. The vibrating collar would have been useless by itself.

You have to work on a dog's attitude and mood first, before you can give him commanding signals and expect him to comply.

Hand Feeding

What are all the qualities you seek from your dog, your companion? This is a question I ask my clients when we begin training. These are the answers most commonly given: not to fight other dogs, not to run away, to come back when called, not to jump up on visitors, to be quiet at home. Hmm. Look at all these negatives. Answers like these make me suspect that the owners don't want a dog but a stuffed bear or a goldfish.

If you attend one of my puppy training classes you'll get a completely different set of answers: friendly, healthy, easy to live with, obedient, confident, happy, flexible, easy to train, keen, loyal, brave, respectful, social, gentle, *well-behaved*, to name a few. When I hear answers like this I know I have an audience that understands what owning a dog is all about: a happy relationship between owner and dog.

Great. That's *our* point of view as humans. Now look at it from your dog's. Why should he want to be clever, obedient, and friendly? What does it all mean to him? Life is full of wonderful things to do, like pursuing joggers in the park, biting passing bicycle tyres, rolling in fox muck, barking at squirrels up a tree and crashing picnics. They soon discover millions of other things to do, creative antics that often offer lots of material for TV shows. These are amusing to watch but it's not so much fun living with a dog that may have eaten, for instance, through a wall and into a neighbour's living room or bitten through an electric wire.

Why should your dog want to do anything you ask him to or behave well according to your expectations? What's in it for him? I hate to tell you, a breezy 'Good boy!' or a pat on his head isn't going to do it for him unless ... and here's the drum roll ... *you* are all these great exciting things. You have to establish yourself as your dog's main provider of food, fun, comfort and guidance – all the good things in his life rolled up into one. In addition, you have to be a bit cleverer than him. You have to know what you're dealing with, get equipped with knowledge and the tools of the trade, and always be one step ahead of him.

How can you do this? I believe that Hand Feeding is the best way to create the qualities you want to see in your dog as early as possible. It is the best way to establish his attention, dependency, concentration, manipulability, loyalty and future trainability. It is the first and most important of your training building blocks. Without establishing yourself as your dog's leader, instructor and overall fount of all pleasures, the rest of your training can't be successfully accomplished. You have to get your dog to both literally and metaphorically *eat out of the palm of your hand.*

Hand Feeding means what it says – feeding your dog from your hand. You simply get rid of his feeding bowl – temporarily – to teach him to become motivated to learn.

The owner of one of my rescued trainees, a dog from an RSPCA centre, told me after an introductory lecture on Hand Feeding, 'Misty has always been eating from my hand. She just refuses to eat from her bowl so we have to nurture her manually; it is her obedience and behaviour with other dogs and off the lead that we don't like.' Well, as you'll see, they hadn't grasped at first the concept and the reason behind the Hand Feeding routine. This owner's take on it is exactly the opposite of what I'm trying to teach you.

Jay starts his Hand Feeding training.
His bowl will be out of the picture for the next few weeks.

Hand Feeding is the basic and principal technique that we use at the Good Boy Dog School, and it is a very short-term routine. There are those who will see dramatic differences in their dog's attitude within a few days, while others will want to persist with the process for a couple of weeks to achieve the results they are seeking. The length of the training period and the time required is entirely dependent on both your and your dog's skill.

This is an excellent way to help you to establish the right working relationship with your dog and to educate him in a way that is natural, easy to follow, comprehensive and stimulating for him. As well as being logical, Hand Feeding is gradual, affordable and quick for you. The moment that you feel you have struck gold and succeeded in getting your dog to respond on a regular basis to your requests, the process can be terminated, although I do suggest using it for reinforcement and maintenance purposes now and then as needed.

Hand Feeding can be used at any stage of your dog's development. It is universally applicable to all dogs – mongrel or pedigree, puppy or adult rescue dog, of any age – as long as he is healthy of body and mind. Naturally, it is always easier to start afresh with a puppy than an older dog, especially one that has suffered traumatic events. But you *can* teach an old dog new tricks! All dogs can be *awakened* and turned on to the practice of Hand Feeding as a basis for training, as it offers them such satisfying rewards. It gives them a chance to change their attitude, to become keen to train. This opportunity is so convincing, it's irresistible.

You have to remember, of course, that every dog, just like us, has its limits. But the earlier your dog can be offered the chance to use his mind, the more he'll be able to achieve. It's most advantageous to start Hand Feeding your new rescue dog the moment you bring him home, while puppies are mentally ready to start as early as four weeks if not earlier, as previously discussed. Regardless of your dog's age, you can always benefit from some guidance and advice from professionals or others knowledgeable about dogs, to make sure you're on the best possible footing before you begin practising.

When you expect your dog to do – or not to do – something for you, ask yourself, 'Why should my dog want to follow my instructions?' 'Because he wants to please me,' you might say. I'm sorry to have to break it to you – and I'll do this as gently as I can – but dogs don't do as we ask because they love us and want to please us. They *do* want to please – but just themselves. I can practically hear you taking in your breath in disbelief. It's a shock, I know, but don't worry, from here on in it's all good news. One of the ways in which we can allow our dogs to please themselves is by keeping us happy too. We participate in a ritual of maintaining a happy medium for both parties – an exchange of favours, in fact. The principle of Hand Feeding is one such way to motivate our dogs to play along, to get involved and be engaged.

Dogs are natural predators and active hunters or scavengers. They hunt or forage in order to maintain and sufficiently support themselves and the members of their pack or family – in short, to survive. They have all the instincts and capabilities built in to achieve these goals, and they are determined to succeed. Their instincts are their guide as well as their lifeline.

Dogs have the strength and stamina to remain on the run for up to 30 hours at a time, and in some cases even longer. They can live without eating for days. They have to search, chase, fight, kill and eat their prey, all of which is incredibly hard work. But they are designed for this. The energy preserved in their little bodies is enough to put them through hell and bring them back in one piece. But it's not just that they *must* do all this; they have the determination and drive to do this much hard work. I know you're thinking that there is no way the sweet, adorable dog cuddling in your lap still hears the call of the wild – but he does!

Is it any wonder then that your hound refuses to come back or stop in mid-hunt while out on a walk? Should we be surprised that he likes to give a good chase to joggers or cyclists in the park or that he demolishes your home and barks constantly when you're out? I want you to be very clear about this. This is what dogs do if they aren't offered a natural, more comprehensive and stimulating alternative. Without us motivating them in more positive, acceptable directions, dogs form bad habits that only get worse over time. They believe 'If it worked for me yesterday, I'll do it again, today!' – thereby perpetuating their bad behaviour.

Dogs aren't houseplants that just need to be watered and fed regularly. They are animals with much more complex needs and desires. They can't sit around doing nothing all day. Therefore we shouldn't expect them to automatically understand what we want from them and to be good according to our rules. To expect otherwise is pure fantasy and projection on our part.

It is very common to hear from dog owners that their dog is perfectly behaved, *except when…*, and they'll reel off various things, like except when a squirrel runs by, except when a bike zips past or except when another dog is around. What owners don't appreciate is that that one thing, whatever it is, is probably indicative of a larger problem that they might not want to admit to or even know about. Many live in a false hope that when their dog ran off this morning for the first time, this will never happen again. That his biting the postman, as he did yesterday – although he's never done it before – will magically go away on its own. It won't, unless you're proactive and do something about it now, and the sooner the better before that 'one-off' becomes a bad habit.

I want to encourage you to dig deeper than just 'How do I get my dog to let go of that man's trousers?' I want to show you that there is another path, one that's totally different once put into practice. There is another way to train and motivate your dog: Hand Feeding. The idea of delivering your dog's food by hand in exchange for his good will and good intentions can't fail. When your dog realises that this is the only alternative he is left with, he'll see obeying you, even if you're the world's biggest softie, as his essential duty.

You shouldn't be too surprised that good dog training boils down to setting goals, motivating and diverting your dog's energy into positive directions, and taking small steps, steadily building to success. After all, we're just the same, are we not? When we want to successfully accomplish something in life, whether it is career or personal goals, we do the same: we plan what we want to accomplish and how we can meet these goals. We give ourselves rewards for reaching important points on that journey, and we try to think positively to reach our destination. Now that you and your dog have enrolled in our training programme, you'll need to keep these basic principles of success in mind as you go through each session – until you're ready to progress to more advanced techniques of communication, of which there are plenty, thanks to the modern science of dog training.

How much food does your dog require?

Ever consider what they must think of us? I mean, here we come
back from a grocery store with the most amazing haul – chicken, pork,
half a cow. They must think we're the greatest hunters on earth!
Anne Tyler

Studies show that 50% of dogs in the UK and USA are overweight, with the majority of their owners not even realising it. And, like people, overweight dogs are at risk from a myriad of health conditions, ranging from poor response reactions to heart disease and diabetes.

Ollie

Therefore it is vital that you determine how much food your dog actually needs before starting on the Hand Feeding programme. You don't want to overfeed, just as you don't wish to underfeed, for any prolonged time. There are plenty of books on nutrition and, of course, your vet can advise you on your dog's weight. But to determine how much a dog actually requires, I like to begin by using standard charts for a dog's breed and size. Then you can:

1. Measure out your dog's food for the day.
2. Divide the food by how many times you feed your dog. If you feed him once, this step is not necessary. If twice, divide by two, and so on.
3. Put your dog's meal down. Let him eat, and after he's stopped, take his bowl away. Some believe that their dog requires as much as 30 minutes to eat, but I personally believe a few minutes – or a few seconds for some ferocious eaters – will do the trick. The moment a dog leaves his bowl, he is done.
4. Measure any food not eaten.
5. Repeat this for every meal for about a week until you determine the proper amount of food your dog actually consumes (you'll need to take into account hot weather, when dogs generally eat less, as well as cold, when they eat more).
6. After you have worked out the proper amount of food your dog needs daily, estimate the amount of his food that makes up a week's ration of equal portions. If you feed your dog once a day, that's seven equal portions; 14 if you feed your dog twice a day; 21 if you feed your dog three times a day, and so on. The food companies may blame me for not letting you waste food, but I think your dog's health is more important, don't you? Always keep an eye on his weight and condition once you've got started. As you get to know his needs, you'll be the best judge of whether or not he's getting enough or too much food. You may want to weigh your dog once a week to have a clear idea of his weight and any fluctuations. In this way you'll be able to adjust the amount of food he require more precisely.

Take away the feeding bowl

Believe me when I tell you that I've seen all manner of misguided ways in which well-intentioned and loving owners care for their dogs. The most popular mistake is to leave a dog's food out all day for him to dine from at his leisure. Let me tell you a story of how such a habit can lead to extremely bad behaviour in your dog.

I was once asked to look at a basset hound who belonged to a Russian pop star. The dog was a large male who lived in a big comfortable house, right next to a huge park. His family was very well off and had plenty of time to give him everything he wanted. And did.

He was very well taken care of; a little too well, in fact. He had five beds of his own, although he never used them, preferring the family's sofa and beds. He had masses of toys lying about the house, most of which he ignored. And the *pièce de résistance*? He had a large crystal bowl about two feet in diameter that sat on the floor and was filled with biscuits of both the dog and human variety. He always ate at his leisure as much as he liked.

The owner's complaints? The dog refused to go for walks when there were visitors in the house; he protested noisily if he was left in another room by himself; and he enjoyed lying under tables biting anyone who put their hand underneath or even moved their feet. He would also attack guests as they tried to sit down, walk in or out of the room or even come around a corner. The family had no shortage of guests, so you can imagine how often the dog could perform his antics.

And why was he doing this? Because he had trained his family to let him do anything he wanted and to supply him with food at all times. What was the best and most efficient way to readjust this dog's thinking, not to mention his owners'? I instructed them to take away his feeding bowl, thus beginning the process of educating him that he is truly dependent on his owner for his food.

I often hear new clients tell me their dog is a fussy eater. The fussy dog is one that either leaves his food untouched or leaves it for some time before going back to it. He is the alpha dog in the mixed, human-dog pack that occupies that home. In a free-living pack of dogs, only the top dog has the privilege of leaving his food and returning to it as he wishes. By allowing him to feed at will, a finicky dog's owner has unwittingly granted him this licence.

The fussy eater is making up the rules, instead of his owner. He knows that his food will remain untouched by human hands until he is good and ready to eat. But fussy eating is a *learned* habit, and a bad one. One hundred per cent of all healthy pups as young as $3^1/_2$–4 weeks respond to food perfectly well. By the age of five months a good third of all puppies show less interest in the treats offered them than we'd like to see. There's nothing wrong with these puppies, they've just become master manipulators. Puppies are mad about food, as we'd expect them to be, but through *our* bad habits and misinformation we create and perpetuate bad eating habits.

Hand Feeding can be the perfect solution for fussy eaters. They'll soon learn you no longer have patience for this type of behaviour. It needs to stop right here and now, as this is where your dog's training foundations begin. For now, put away your dog's feeding bowl, or, as Dr Ian Dunbar says, throw it away! It's getting in the way of establishing a good and healthy relationship between you and your dog. It's confusing your communication channels. Soon you'll be able to go back to a regular feeding programme. For now, though, put that bowl away!

If you have any concerns about the Hand Feeding process, by all means consult your vet or a knowledgeable dog person. They will tell you that by using a little tough love in not letting your dog decide when he's ready to eat, you'll actually enable him to reach his ideal weight. If he isn't hungry because his food is always available, you won't be able to have any control over his weight. By gaining control of his eating habits by successfully following the Hand

Feeding regime, you'll succeed in getting him to agree to eat all that you put in his feeding bowl when you put it down once more.

Now, instead of putting your dog's bowl out for him at a designated time, you're going to begin Hand Feeding him his food for ten days to two weeks, or longer at your discretion. But remember, Hand Feeding is a *temporary* training device.

Practically speaking, it is easier to use dry food. You can use tinned or preserved food, but as it's a little messier, get yourself some hand wipes or rubber gloves.

You can Hand Feed your dog anywhere – in front of the TV while watching your favourite soaps, in the garden, outside on your walks, or in the park in front of playing dogs and children, which you'll have to do when the time comes. Make yourself comfortable. In time, make sure Hand Feeding works everywhere you have time to do it.

Over the following ten sessions you'll be learning everything you need to teach your dog – nearly any act you can think of that a dog is capable of performing. The whole canine repertoire will be covered as you follow our instructions from start to finish.

The sessions are to be done at your own pace. Here I must stress again: be careful to not go too fast. It's better to get the rudiments down solidly than have to start a session again from scratch when you hit a major snag.

Session 1: A fresh start

Today you're taking your first steps in learning how to communicate, cooperate and coordinate with your dog. So here we go...

Take your allocated ration and place a small bite of your dog's food in the palm of your hand. Allow him to move towards it and take the food. Start by putting your hand just half an inch from his mouth. *You're looking for him to make an effort to come to you and take the food.* If he doesn't, put the food away and try again at the next mealtime. If he does come to you, continue to feed him his entire meal from the palm of your hand. I normally give a dog a few chances at the start, but soon you'll know exactly what to expect from yours. Note that most dogs will do this quite easily and find this no challenge at all.

However, other dogs, such as mistreated rescue dogs, are so distrustful that even such a simple exercise fills them with anxiety. There are timid animals, ones that have simply never taken anything from a human before, and many other types. In such cases you may need to scatter the food on the floor in front of you and even leave the room before he'll eat. In this type of situation you need to build a basic level of trust that is entirely absent.

It may take a few days, maybe a bit longer. But, in the end, his appetite will help you win him over. Take it slowly, proceed cautiously. Take the smallest of steps as you move about. When he is comfortable eating the food you've scattered on the floor for him, try staying in the same room – maybe keeping to the opposite end. Relax, read a book and ignore him. Let him eat. Your relaxed demeanour will help him to relax.

When he's succeeded in eating while in the same room with you, the next step is to draw him closer by scattering his food gradually nearer to you until, finally, he is taking it straight from your hand. This is very reminiscent of the film *Dances with Wolves*, where the main character, played by Kevin Costner, tames a wolf. It takes nearly half the movie for the wolf to trust him – all accomplished by offering the animal food from a safe distance, building trust and drawing him closer and closer in. The feeder's hand became something for the wolf to look forward to and therefore created a positive association. It may be just a film, but it demonstrates perfectly the way to build trust.

If your dog isn't being distrustful, just being his normal finicky self, and he won't take the food from you, put it away until the next mealtime. If he refuses to eat at the next mealtime, withhold his food once more. Don't worry, he won't starve. Dogs can, and actually often do, go a few days without eating without any bodily harm, but you should *never* withhold water.

Good training makes for happier dogs.

Most of my clients find this particular brand of tough love much harder for them than it is for their dog. Just ask Emily, who has had a very difficult time because her Jack Russell is Kate Moss waif-thin (causing Emily to feel sorry for her) and has the capacity to whine ceaselessly if she doesn't get what she wants when she wants it (causing Emily to give her what she wants just to restore peace; lucky dog). But rest assured, your dog will get hungry eventually, and the next time you present his food he'll take it and won't turn up his nose at you and food ever again. A hard lesson for both of you perhaps, but an important one if you are to continue to be successful in your training.

What if your dog will only eat half of his food, or just a third? Put the food away and don't offer any until the next meal, when you should offer him only the amount he ate previously. The next time, give him his full amount again. If he still refuses to eat all his food, repeat the exercise. But once he has accepted the *challenge*, slowly begin to top up his food with what he missed out on, just to allow him to catch up with that desired quantity.

Admittedly, there are some slower-thinking dogs that may take longer to appreciate this new scenario than others who may grasp it in a minute. Give a dog like this some extra time and simply start by putting the feeding bowl in new places, or by placing his food inside of some shell from which he'll have to winkle out his food – for instance, a Kong toy, Activity Ball, used yogurt pot or Buster Cube (though the last may be very hard for some dogs to master). Once your dog has developed an *open-mindedness* about where his food comes from, he is ready to start working with you and to learn to take food from your hand.

I have, by the way, successfully used the Hand Feeding principle on other animals. One recent Christmas we found an abandoned parrot perched on our driveway. We brought him inside and tried to find out who his owner was, but no one claimed him. So he became ours and we named him Christopher. In the first few days that we had him I spent the time investigating the level of contact he had had with humans. It appeared to be nil. But it wasn't just that he was uninterested in communicating with us or uneducated; he was frightened and shy and wholly opposed to any suggestion of interaction with me. A perfect candidate for Hand Feeding.

When we first began he would flee to the opposite side of his cage and wouldn't even touch his food until I was a good distance away. But I was delighted to see that it only took a few days to get him to feed from my hand, and, not only that, feed from my hand while sitting on it too. I had never before tried the Hand Feeding technique on a bird, aside from the crows that like to sit in on my one-to-one dog training. Using treats, we get them to squawk, hop in a circle, walk towards us and stay, fly and sit on a bench and even play ball. And no, the dogs don't run after them. They are given more positive things to think about.

As soon as your dog gets the hang of taking his food from you, you can proceed to make it fun. Fun? Remember, in the wild, dogs have to find their own food. It's their main activity, their main challenge for the day, right up there with finding a drink of water or a comfy place to sleep. Dogs need a challenge. They're hard-wired for it. They get badly bored if they don't have some form of stimulating activity, and any of you who has a dog that likes to chew up your things when you're out all day will know what I'm talking about. So why not make mealtimes a bit of a challenge too? This will become a good-for-his-brain activity that he'll find stimulating and therefore eminently satisfying. You'll see how hooked he gets on the emotional satisfaction and the pleasure of success.

You started off by placing your dog's food in the palm of your hand, just a few inches away from him, and getting him to come towards your hand to collect his reward. You may be growing bored and thinking, OK, this genius in front of me has got this down pat, now what? But look what you've already achieved. You're already mastering teaching your dog to be gentle around your hands, to 'soft-mouth', as well as to grow dependent on you.

You're teaching your dog to *want* to cooperate with you. Think of it this way: the next time he picks up a disgusting piece of decayed fried chicken abandoned at the side of the road and you want him to leave it, the Hand Feeding method will help you to get him to do exactly that. There's a big pay-off here, so keep at it.

Let's continue. Say you're already halfway through your dog's dinner (he's the one eating, not you). Now, with you remaining still – that is, sitting – move the food an inch to the right. Let him follow your hand and collect his reward. Then the same, an inch to the left. Then an inch up, an inch down. Try switching hands, encouraging him to go from left to right, or even in a small semicircle. In your first session together, the furthest distance that I recommend you present his food from is 10–15 inches, however confident you may feel.

Make sure that whatever you're asking him to do you build only from a level where your dog is comfortable. It's better to spend more time doing the groundwork properly than to have the entire empire of your dog's obedience collapse at a later stage. Some dogs' attention span and concentration skills are non-existent. But after a couple of sessions of eating from the palm of your hand, you'll motivate your student to stay with you until the final school bell rings, so to speak, acknowledging the end of the session – and the last of his meal.

Has he got it? Great. Now, let's up the challenge.

Session 2: Playing conductor

In this session you're standing while your dog is doing all the walking. You're conducting while he plays to your tune. Adjust your height so that your hand is level with his nose. Extend your arm out to the right with a titbit. Give him time to follow your arm out. When he does, give him his reward. Do the same to the left. Now up, treat, then down, treat. Right, treat, left, treat, up, treat, down, treat. Right, treat, up, treat, down, treat, left, treat. Mix it up and keep those rewards flowing.

Now let's really be daring. While you're still standing, bend as needed and guide your dog in a wide circle in front of you. Make sure that the treat is close up to his nose – or his nose to the treat – and guide him slowly. No need to make him dizzy. Look at that. He's *twirling*. My friend Val has a terrier-cross, Miri, who is a show-stopping twirler and can do about five different varieties – like standing on her back legs and hopping in a circle, twirling in place and so on. This, combined with her good looks and posing expertise, has gained her stardom in the *Daily Mail*, the National Canine Defence League and *Dogs Today* magazine's 2003 calendar. But for now, you and your dog can be very pleased with a basic twirl. When you've mastered a few more advanced skills you can begin to create your own variations and experiment.

Val and her terrier-cross, Miri.

Another important step forward in this session is a more advanced and technically complicated kind of 'following' routine. By now you're great at sending your dog from one side to another and from back to front and back again. But don't stop there. Go back to placing a biscuit at his nose level. You'll need to move very slowly and make sure that he is pressing or leaning into your hand at all times in this exercise. Make the same movements as above, but only a few inches to start with, being very precise. Go left – your dog is almost hanging off your hand. Reward, then move slowly back, dog in full contact. Again, be precise – it's either yes or no, good or bad, black or white. Dogs don't think in half measures. Continue steady and clear, weave left and right, around one way and then the other, keeping your dog glued to your leading hand.

You want your dog's undivided attention, don't you? Nothing grabs it better than one of the easiest and most enjoyable games around. Chuck a biscuit up in the air and give him a chance to catch it. He's not good at it, you say? Nonsense, it's you who isn't good at it! Start throwing the treats low and close to your dog, then build up the height. At our parties we have a little doggie competition where handlers leave their dogs at a starting line and take one step backwards in front of them. They toss a treat to the dogs, and if their dog catches it, they can take another step back and toss a further titbit. If a dog misses, he and his owner are out. It's a simple game but it requires skill and coordination from both handler and dog.

By coincidence, this little game also sharpens your dog's listening and watching skills. Dogs with better catching skills are often better listeners. Their owners are able to deliver their messages faster, as their dogs are used to listening and watching them. So, as you can see, this is a game well worth playing, either on your own with your dog or in a group.

Well done. In your next session you'll begin to imitate actual recognised commands. But don't jump ahead until your dog has regularly enjoyed his food while following your arm movements. Feel free to take a break for a few days until you're ready to tackle more.

Clicker training

While you're practising, here's a little more information about clicker training which we mentioned earlier as an optional training tool. You may find it's just the thing to move your training along at a steady clip.

The clicker, found in most pet stores, is a small object that fits easily into the palm of your hand and is simple to use once you know how. You click the clicker and treat your dog when he acts in a positive manner. He'll learn rapidly to expect to receive a treat every time he hears the click. If you and your dog want to work side by side to reach new horizons, the clicker will be your friend, helping to push you beyond your limits and to speed up the process exponentially.

But the clicker isn't a magic wand and won't be useful if not employed correctly with a full understanding of its operation and value. The BBC showed a programme called *Celebrity Dog School* in which three out of the seven trainers on the show used a clicker to train a dog to do a specific task. It was obvious that two of them didn't have a clear idea of how the clicker works. Dogs were forced to perform tasks and pulled by their leads, and none actually looked forward to learning or achieving any results apart from trying to get away. And this was supposed to be valuable to the general public?

Clickers have finally become widely known and used – which is great – and are very trendy among professional dog trainers. But many of these haven't done their homework properly, and many novices aren't getting the necessary training in their proper use. Clickers, I repeat, aren't magic; they can't transform an untrained dog into an attentive pupil, especially if he hasn't learned to be reward-dependent. They are, instead, an advanced communication tool; a kind of canine dictionary for dogs that are keen and thirsty for knowledge.

Clicker training doesn't require a clicker *per se*. The device is simply a way of exchanging messages of a very precise and comprehensive nature. Clicker-trained dogs are good dogs in the first place – happy to be told what to do, keen to learn and willing to try or follow up on the handler's cues, however small they might be.

I love using this method, and many, if not all, of my advanced trainees are clicker-trained. But they weren't trained in this way from the start. First, as we do in our Hand Feeding programme, their owners worked on establishing some kind of connection with their dogs. Then they widened their repertoires and attitude margins, and expanded their dogs' manoeuvrability and manipulability.

It is only during these later stages that you should introduce the clicker as a 'secondary reinforcer'. You offer food, as the 'primary reinforcer', to your dog as a reward for his good response. Food used in this way marks the particular behaviour that you wish to encourage, so it becomes obvious to him exactly what is expected out of all his catalogue of moves.

Let's say you ask your dog to sit and after he's tried to jump for his treat, chew it out of your hand or given up and walked away (or one of many other things), he then sits down and gets rewarded at that very moment. What is he going to do after a bit of practice, experimenting and attempts? He's more likely to sit for you, just as instructed. This is known as 'shaping'.

But, being human and imperfect, we often don't reward in the most precise way. Delivering that reward often coincides with various other acts from your dog, like looking away, lifting a paw, getting up or lowering his body, stretching or yawning. In this case these acts are what you're reinforcing − not your requested positioning − and this is why trainers with better timing have less confused, quicker-responding and more easily trained dogs.

Therefore it is vital to sharpen your reaction time, as the clearer the message you send, the more precise and obvious trace it will leave in your dog's mind. Imagine taking a snapshot of your dog pressed up to your leg as you're walking together and giving him a reward at that precise moment. Would he understand the message if he was taught to learn in this way? Easily. Without it, you're hardly going to see such a result and even if you do, it may only last for a split second. To catch it with a reward − even if this is already in your left hand near your dog's mouth − is going to be a tough job. You may have to act as if you were in a combat situation and, as the unexpected is likely to strike at any moment, you must react instantaneously as your whole success depends on it! So how do you do it?

Karen Pryor, the initiator of the clicker training method, came up with the idea of 'click and treat' while working with dolphins, as forcing them to do anything would be quite a challenge, I think you'll agree. It's the same with dogs. So, at the time your dog's action even remotely reminds you of the one you're after, you click and treat. The click pinpoints the most desirable moment of the presented repertoire, so there's minimum confusion about what your dog should do. The treat, the compulsory part of the clicker training routine, makes it all work, because it isn't the click your dog is after but the actual reward. I'll say it again: *food is the primary reinforcer and unconditional stimulus that motivates your dog to work and remember things.*

But the reward and your dog's response have to be associated with each other. While you're Hand Feeding you achieve this when he is looking for clues and hints on what you're waiting for him to do. Don't even attempt to introduce the clicker any earlier. But, once ready, start by clicking (a single click) from a distance – holding the clicker in your pocket or behind your back – just a second or so before you deliver the next portion of titbits, then treat and repeat, again. About two weeks later (on average) your dog may actually notice there is a clicker in the chain of events: request – behaviour – click – treat, and only after that, can your dog start concentrating on that click and where and when it sounds.

The above describes just the short and introductory phase for this magnificent, extraordinarily useful and effective gadget. The clicker can be used for teaching many behaviours, as well as for correcting undesirable habits, by simply clicking and treating your dog for not doing the things you want him to stop doing. Apart from being an immensely sharp messenger, the clicker helps you to bring new elements into your training, and as novelty often does, it will intrigue your dog and form a clear and brand-new idea of training in his mind.

Of course, there are some limitations, for there are no perfect solutions. Clicker training can be later combined with or replaced by other techniques or even abandoned altogether as the results it achieves become permanently learned.

There has been much research, and many wonderful manuals have been published, on clicker training, and I especially recommend those by Gary Wilkes and Karen Pryor (see Bibliography, p.252). They have written the gospels of clicker training and you'll need to read them before you can begin seriously to consider using a clicker.

Session 3: These boots were made for walking

Now it's time to get both you and your dog walking. Most of the moves you'll be doing with him in this session will remind you of one command or another. And even if you're a complete novice, the skills you and your dog will be developing here will certainly help you later to transfer them into something more complicated. On top of everything your dog will gain the most powerful tools in dog training: *good will, the right attitude, a keen approach and a strong want.* This is what will take all the effort. The rest is peanuts.

Hard to believe? Do you consider your dog's problems are too severe for such a gentle approach? Well, what better way to find out than to try? You have already invested in reading this book, so just go with the flow and experiment. Begin again at your dog's next mealtime. Take a step back, moving your hand back with you, with your dog's food in it, towards your knees. If you have a large breed, you'll want to move your hands higher up to his nose level. You move back – he follows, you bring your hands near into your body, he comes to you.

Recognise this? This is the basics of 'recall' training – teaching your dog to come to you – as well as the 'present' position – getting your dog to sit closely in front of you. We'll go into these in more detail in Session 6.

Now try a bit more moving around together. Spin on the spot – a quarter-turn one way, and give him a bit of his dinner when he follows. Make a quarter-turn the other way and again give him a portion of food as he keeps up with you. Half a step one way – reward; half a step the other – reward.

Now try a 180-degree turn, keeping your hand – holding a treat – level with his nose. Treat when he follows. Now 180 degrees the other way, reward.

You see something familiar here? These moves are the basics of 'heelwork' – teaching your dog to watch, listen and follow you (rather than the other way around). Eye-opening, isn't it? I get excited every time I get a dog to go this far. I feel he is mine. No more than I am his, though. We're bonding, agreeing on playing teacher and pupil. We're communicating.

The basics of heelwork involve getting your dog to follow a treat, then your hand, your arm, and then finally you. Getting your dog to stay close to your side is one of the hardest positions to teach, because of its emphasis on leadership. It's also the most confusing exercise because, unlike positions such as 'sit' and 'stay', 'heel' doesn't have an automatic ending. When does a dog know he doesn't have to heel any more? It's all up to you to communicate with and to lead your dog.

It doesn't matter what side you choose to keep your dog, left or right, or the exact position in the beginning. The first stage of heelwork is 'interactive following' – building up the distance and terrain, and varying it every way you can. However, it is best to decide which side you wish your dog to walk beside you. Traditionally in Britain, it is taught to keep your dog to your left side. This was adopted from police dog handling, where the dog is to the left to keep the right arm free for using a weapon. But for us pet owners, whether it's left or right is inconsequential. We just don't want the dog making the decision for us.

Now begin to walk. Holding a new treat in your hand and down by your side, reward your dog each time he makes an effort to catch up with you and eventually presses his nose to your hand – that is to say, every time he stays close to and even with your chosen leg. Continue to practise this, always replenishing the treats in your hand so that you can reward him at regular intervals, even if you have to start with every five seconds. When you wish to make the exercise a little more difficult, begin to change speed or direction. Walk straight a few paces, then make a sharp but not too fast turn to one side. Give your dog a moment to catch up as you continue to walk, and then treat him when he is in the correct position by your side. Then make a turn the other way and repeat. Remember to keep rewarding him with titbits all the way.

Next, start to walk in a zigzag or in a tight circle; try to play hard to get, but don't turn too fast or run too quickly, as the most common problem with heelwork training is a dog's failure to anticipate his owner's moves. Slow down, keep mixing up your turns, but allow your dog time to catch up, otherwise you'll only frustrate and confuse him. He'll soon learn that you don't always go in the same direction (straight) and that he'd better pay attention or he'll get stepped on or left behind. As your dog begins to understand what's required of him, you can attach a verbal command to the heel positioning: 'heel', 'with me', 'close', or whatever you like.

Using your clicker is especially useful for teaching heelwork because, as mentioned previously, you can capture an exact movement and moment in time that you want your dog to remember. 'Click and treat' is the most effective and fastest way of teaching this. Later you can experiment by using no bribe of any kind. But be alert, while clicking, for the moves that remind you of the correct position you desire.

'Walking on the lead' follows the same pattern of teaching as heel-work, so try not to show any difference in your training of it. Keep a loose lead and encourage your dog to follow you. Some see walking on the lead as less demanding of the dog, as all we want him to do is not pull you down the road or jerk you from left to right. Walking on the lead is all about him following you, and not the other way around. Just like the previous exercise, this can be a more relaxed positioning for your dog. He may not be required to stick right by your side – but if he wants to, that's great. Balance it yourself, but don't compromise. We want the dog to follow your intentions, not you his. It's dangerously easy, as many of you probably know, to give in a little and then before you know it, you've lost all control.

First, teaching your dog to walk properly on the lead is essential, as there may be circumstances where he is required by law to be on a lead, for instance on public roads. Second, even if this is not required where you are, it's the responsible thing to do while on or near streets, car parks or other possible dangers. Even the best-trained dog can be startled and placed in danger if not on a lead, so don't take risks with your dog's life or the lives of others.

Ready? Attach the lead to your dog's collar and follow the same routine as before. Make sure your dog is on the same side as when you taught him to heel, so as not to confuse him. Now begin walking with a loose lead – that is, don't try to get him to walk nicely by shortening the lead, restricting his movements (he'll pull just as much on a short lead as on a long). Lead work is a complicated skill. It isn't truly learned properly until you've introduced distractions (which we will cover shortly) and polished it up with other techniques. But this is how you first begin.

Is your dog walking nicely, not pulling you this way and that? Probably not. He may only be walking well for a few seconds at a time. When he does walk calmly by your side, reward him. The two of you want to enjoy it, don't you? But how can you if you're constantly badgering him to stop pulling by yanking on his lead? Instead, send him a different message – one of reward – when he does as you wish. Even if he is only walking well for a few seconds at a time, reward him during that time. Gradually, those few seconds will turn into ten, then 20, 30, then always.

Practise patience and persistence. This is the one exercise where people are most likely to lose their cool. But just as yelling at a traffic warden for giving you a ticket won't stop them from issuing you one, so losing your temper with your dog won't help you to train him. Remember, Meg isn't yanking you from one side of the pavement to the other just to irritate you; she's doing it because she can and she hasn't been taught to walk any other way.

Furthermore, walking on the lead doesn't have to be all about walking from point A to point B. You can spice it up by adding elements you've already learned. Anything you do that reinforces your dog's need to look to you for guidance will help you train him to walk properly on the lead. Try alternating a slow and a fast pace, zigzagging along the pavement, taking a few sharp turns, and using a variety and versatility of rewards. (I'll show you more tips of heelwork and lead work in Management solutions, p. 192.)

Now mix and match all that you've done today. Dogs are clever, but if your training routine gets more and more complicated while he makes only modest progress, he'll say, 'Enough! I'll play stupid!' and won't go along. To counteract the attitude 'the harder I try, the harder it gets, so I'll just run off now and see how the squirrels are doing in the yard', vary the level of challenges, making it harder and then going back to kindergarten.

Sounds too simple? But look what you've already achieved. You have already promoted your dog from the basic level of 'every dog can do it' to a more advanced one where he gets his reward and looks up to *you* for the next one. He's got one task under his belt and is already looking forward to the next one. In my opinion, a good dog is one that always looks to you in anticipation of something because he never feels like he knows it all. (Neither do we, of course, but we can't let on.)

Now you both deserve a break. Wash your hands, wipe off the drool, sweep up the floor, dry off your dog's beard, make up with your partner for the time you have taken off your house duties, phone your friends to catch up, and get on with your life... until the next meal. See you there.

Doushman in the snow

Chapter 5
Step 2: Word Games

The great pleasure of a dog is that you may make a fool
of yourself with him and not only will he not scold you,
but he will make a fool of himself too.
Samuel Butler (1835–1902)

STEP 2:
WORD GAMES

There are plenty of fine books that go through the basics of obedience training, 'sit', 'stay' and so on, and by all means further supplement your reading with whatever you feel will help. In Step 2 I'll give you a more organic way of instructing your dog than is traditionally taught.

I don't much like the word 'command' to describe the activities we're going to be doing with your dog. It's too severe. You'll soon discover, if you haven't already, that working with your dog to communicate is a pleasure! So, instead of referring to words like 'sit' or 'stay' as commands, why not call them 'word games' to get ourselves into the spirit of things?

You've already begun to see that your dog's response to food, which is an unconditioned reflex, is slowly being replaced by a conditioned reflex – your hand (and you, of course) start to attract his attention as you and his food always come together, an intertwined pair. According to Pavlov, food – a primary reinforcer – makes it possible for your gestures and movements to be remembered by your dog as secondary (conditional) reinforcers. Once this has been achieved you can begin to add another form of secondary reinforcer – verbal signals. So first your dog needs to attribute food to you, your movements and his responses. Then and only then do I recommend attaching a verbal signal. He has to understand what action is required of him before you can attach a word to it. Otherwise 'sit', for instance, will be meaningless.

One way to train a dog to learn to perform certain moves is to wait for the action to take place and reward your dog when he does it – a reinforcement training method that is widely used by clicker trainers. For instance, wait for your dog to sit. Eventually he'll do so. When he does, reward him. After a while the light will dawn, and he'll begin to sit just to get the reward. When he has finally linked his reward with a sit, you can give it a name. Just before he sits, you say, 'Sit', wait for him to accomplish the act and then reward him. Eventually, you'll be able to take the final step and ask him to sit and get the desired result.

Dogs are visual animals. Their sense of smell is also vital, but about 90–95% of information they receive is through their eyes. Also, a deaf dog is far less handicapped than a blind one. So why teach your dog words? By building up his vocabulary, you're able to open his mind to your suggestions and make him cleverer in a socially accepted way. Also, he can't always see what you're asking him to do, but will be able to hear you or a sound signal you transmit, like a whistle, in some situations. By learning words, your dog will be able to cope with most of life's challenges. And if he is rewarded consistently for his consistent compliance, there will be fewer misunderstandings and less confusion. Consequently, your dog will actually learn to look forward to the next instruction, whether it be visual or verbal.

There are many words you can teach your dog to respond to and understand. The basic ones I'll demonstrate here will get you started and will put into play the various ways you can teach your dog to understand word games (some you may even make up on your own), so that his reactions to your requests in various circumstances become automatic and proficient. Remember that dogs don't speak languages but associate memory with the verbal communication of humans. Therefore they can become multilingual just as easily as learning your commands in English.

Various sources state the learning limit of a dog is between 80 and 180 words. I believe there is practically no limit to the number of words you can teach your dog. It all depends on you and him. It's up to you to stretch your collective limits and, above all, enjoy it. I've never trained in order to prove or disprove these statistics as I've never thought it of any real importance. The purpose of training, in my opinion, isn't to see what kind of levels you can reach on paper but to see how far you and your dog can go to better understand each other. With this will come proficiency, a much more useful yardstick of success.

Training is a lifelong activity. It takes practice, patience and maintenance to keep your dog's responses sharp. The whole process is very similar to our learning a new language. If we don't practise regularly, we either forget what we've learned or we take longer to find the right words for things that otherwise would come easily if we had practised consistently. It's much the same for dogs, despite their superior memories.

Session 4: Cool dog moves

In this session you'll be working on getting your dog to change positions. Don't try to learn all the following in one go. Instead, concentrate on just one or two moves every time you play together.

Grab a bowl or bag filled with a portion of your dog's daily ration and let's get going once more. As always, you can dole out his meal while you're out for a walk, or anywhere you're comfortable in the house. Just this morning I practised all the way to the park with a puppy, dishing out his meal as we went, just so I wouldn't have to be pulled all the way there and back.

Let's go. How about teaching your dog to sit? As mentioned above, you can teach this by waiting for him to sit on his own and then rewarding him. All you do is wait for a sit to happen. This approach can also be applied to teaching a plethora of other words and positions. Another traditional method is to guide your dog into a sit, place a treat directly above his nose and bring it back slightly over his head. This encourages him to sit automatically. Remember, teach the position first, and attach a word to it later, when your dog has learned the movement required.

By lowering a treat to the ground, you can encourage your dog to bow or to stretch. Again, you can just wait for the position to naturally emerge and reward him with a titbit. Repeat this on several occasions, until you're able to apply a word to it. Then he'll be able to bow on request. You're putting a movement to a cue.

Harvey waits for his reward after he demonstrates a stand.

Another great game is teaching your dog to stand. The first part is to teach the position. You won't have long to wait for him to naturally stand on all fours. Treat him. He'll think it's great that he got a treat for doing absolutely nothing. Once you're able to attach the verbal signal 'stand' (or 'up', as 'stand' can sound too similar to 'stay') to the position, you can ask him to stand when he is sitting or lying down. You can also bribe a dog to do it by waiting for him to stand back while he is straightening his hind legs instead of his walking forward into a stand. See for yourself what works better for you and how your dog learns it best.

Next, get your dog to beg – to raise his front paws while keeping his bum on the ground. Have him give you his paw up on your forearm. Try to bribe him up, and as he looks for some support he'll raise his second paw off the ground. Reward him. Continue this exercise, gradually building up to the level where he has brought his second paw up on to your arm. Look at that. He looks like he's sitting at school. Another way to instruct your dog to beg is to put him in the sit position, lift a treat an inch or two above his nose, guiding it slightly back and over his head – somewhere just above the centre of gravity – thereby encouraging him to raise his front paws off the ground. In the initial stages it's enough to have him raise his paws a mere shave off the ground. Praise and treat him. Then gradually become more exacting until he's managed to raise his front paws to his chest level. A dog's sense of balance isn't as inherent as we think. With a bit of persistence, you can develop it to perfection.

The same principle applies to teaching your dog to lie down. Wait until he is lying flat on his belly and reward him, eventually building it to attaching the word 'down' and losing the hand signal. After this you'll be able to ask your dog to lie down when he is in a different position, like sitting.

Barbara and Casper demonstrate down.

Note that it isn't the actual 'down' or 'sit' we're after but more the will from your dog to cooperate – willingness, compliance and effort. At times you'll only be rewarding a part of an exercise, a breakdown of movements. Some tricks or commands may include ten or more stages. 'Lie down', for instance, may be encouraged with a treat for just lowering a head towards your hand, stretching forward a bit, moving back, moving one of his front legs ahead, leaning down and maybe then a full touch down! – a real challenge for insecure, distrustful, stubborn or unhappy-to-submit dogs. 'Down', by the way, is the most subordinate pose, so by practising it in various surroundings you'll improve your dog's perception of other people and other dogs.

Another great command that you can always use to strengthen your training in general is 'Watch me!' In this interaction with your dog, you reward him for his extensive eye contact and attention, thereby reinforcing this highly desirable quality. Click and treat him for the behaviour you're looking for, and it won't take you any time at all to teach it. As we've said and will continue to say, one of the most important aspects of training is gaining your dog's attention and focus. Our Hand Feeding exercises help you achieve this in the most positive way possible for your dog.

Now go back through the movements we've done in our earlier sessions and try to attach a word or two to all of them, like 'here', 'this way', 'go round', 'look up', 'come', 'follow'.

After your dog has learned each individual word, you can begin to string them together into a great repertoire of word games. Ask him to sit; then stand up; then lie down – alternating the moves. Throw in a request for a bow and a beg once in a while too, and everything else you've learned previously. Mix it all up so your dog can't anticipate but instead has to concentrate on the understanding of each request.

Wow! Look what you've achieved. You have a great little routine going now. Every dinnertime you can take your dog through his moves, mixing up the combinations so he can't anticipate what you're going to ask of him. Practise in the park, in the living room, while sitting at a café. Show off. I can't tell you how happy it will make *you* feel when you see how well your dog is doing, and *he* will love the attention from passers-by, which will encourage you both even more.

Session 5: Cuddling up

Here you'll be bringing your dog in for some close interaction – and a lot of fun. This is where all the great experimentation really kicks in and you can create an infinitesimal amount of unique games for you and your dog to play.

We'll start by teaching him to walk in between your legs by placing your feeding hand on the one side of the arch they form, leading him through your legs and marking his progress with reward.

Try to join the moves together while you stand with your legs spread apart – in and around, in the other way and around to the front once more. You may have to be dextrous and move the treat from your left to your right hand, or use one titbit in each hand. Eventually build this up so that your dog is doing a fluid figure of eight from right to left and left to right.

Now that he has got the taste for fancy moves, let's see what else you can challenge him to do. The following are a few of my favourites.

I like beginning this one at home, but you can improvise using whatever props you wish (as long as they are safe). Do it wherever you're most comfortable. Sit down on the floor, facing a wall or piece of furniture, tuck one leg under you and keep the other straight, with your foot to the wall. Make sure this leg is no more than a few inches off the ground to start with. Place your dog on one side and with a treat guide him over your leg. If he's a larger dog, he'll just be stepping over it. If he's a smaller breed, like a toy poodle, he'll be nearly leaping. Now get your dog to turn around and step or jump over your leg from the other side. Do this a few times and when you feel he's comfortable, raise your leg a little higher. Guide him over again. As he goes over, you can begin to use the word 'jump'. Don't forget to give him his reward and tell him how clever he is. Lots of positive affirmation is so important.

This next one is an exercise that you can build on over time. Have you seen those clever dogs jumping through their trainers' arms, or hoops, in the show ring? They all started by first going over small obstacles and then working their way slowly up to higher and higher levels.

Now, instead of having your dog jump over your leg, why not have him crawl underneath? Get in the same position as above, but bring your leg up higher so he'll be less inclined to jump over it. Also, instead of guiding your dog over your leg with the help of a treat, you'll be focusing his attention by offering a treat *underneath* your leg.

As your dog grows comfortable with this game, bring your leg gradually lower so that he has to really crawl to go underneath. As you guide him through, ask him to 'crawl'.

Another technique to teach your dog to crawl is to have him in the 'down' position and drag a treat on the floor out in front of his nose, encouraging him to crawl towards it. You have to move the treat very slowly, otherwise he'll try to stand up to get it.

You can also teach your dog to roll over. Start by getting him in the 'down' position and slowly bribe him to flip to one side, his thigh first. As he looks at your treat, following it with his nose, reward him. As he tries to reach further over, reward him once more. The moment he curls up, flipping his backside, he has rolled over. If he hasn't quite got there, see where his shoulder blade is located and try to follow that line up from the elbow joint to the spinal cord. Don't put the treat any further back than his shoulder, as otherwise he'll simply be able to bend and take the reward on offer.

If you can't get him to follow your hand, go more slowly. Let him feel comfortable with the task. Break up the exercise into stages:

first, lying flat on his side; then trying to reach for your hand and titbit on the other side of his body. Now you have two tricks up your sleeve: lying flat, or 'dead dog', plus 'roll over'.

Gradually, as your dog understands the move he's suppose to be making, you can tell him to roll over as he's doing it, thereby placing a verbal secondary reinforcer on the move. Then slowly start weaning him off the hand signal, just as with most of the other commands. Eventually you'll be able to ask him to do this without having to crouch over him. It can take many weeks of practice, so don't get frustrated if your little genius doesn't pick it up straight away.

Session 6: Gimme five! and other funky moves

In this session you'll be learning how to instruct your dog to give you one paw, then both paws.

As we said earlier, you can always wait for him to give you his paw – many dogs do this while they are begging or trying to get your attention – and reward him every time he does this. Or, if he doesn't do it automatically, you can wait until he raises a paw ever so slightly off the ground and reward him every time. (It's best to focus on just one paw to start with.)

Another option is to let your dog see you place a treat in the palm of your hand, make a fist and place it in front of him. When he raises a paw, no matter how small a movement, treat him. If he goes for your fist right away, trying to paw the treat out of your hand, your job will be easier, but some dogs have better manners than others. If yours is one of the better-mannered ones who barely lift a paw, you'll need to build him up to a full paw position by gradually becoming more demanding. You can also place your fist lower, as this can be helpful, and raise it slowly up to his chest level as he improves. Present a reward, and provided that your dog is really keen, he'll try his best to get it. You may have to put up with the licking and chewing, but most dogs will try to dig it out of your hand in the first couple of minutes if they don't succeed otherwise. As soon as he raises a paw, reward him. Be quick, or you'll miss the moment. Keep practising. When your dog finally has learned what's expected of him, you can put a word to his movements, like 'paw', 'shake' or 'high five'.

You can also teach your dog to 'speak', or bark on command. As with teaching many of the other movements and positions, you wait for the activity to naturally occur – in this instance when he barks – and reward him. In the beginning, the recommended hand signal commonly applied to this action is the same as if you were wearing a hand puppet and moving its mouth with your fingers, open and closed, open and closed. But you can use any signal you choose. With a dog that doesn't bark much, this may be a difficult exercise to accomplish. Some dogs are more vocal than others and make all sorts of noises, grunting, growling and moaning. These are your best candidates, but take heart if your dog is a quiet one. If you're very patient and prepared, you'll be able to teach him to speak. As soon as he understands that he must bark when your hand 'speaks', you can begin by saying 'speak' or 'bark' or whatever you like. A few of our students have a wide repertoire of commands that include everything from a quiet to a loud 'speak', a growl and even 'Mama' or 'Wow!'

How about a bit of dancing? You can teach your dog to walk backwards and forwards in a straight line. The new bit for you, of course, is teaching him to reverse. Place a treat in your fist and place it right underneath his chin. Move your hand an inch or so towards his chest and wait until he moves back in an effort to get the food. He'll naturally walk backwards to try to get at the treat. At first, it's enough if he makes any movements backwards at all. Later you should aim to sharpen his response, rewarding him only when he has gone in a straight line – with or without your hand.

When you want him to walk forward, all you need to do is place a treat in front of his nose and move your hand, or even walk towards him yourself. He'll chase the treat, walking forward. Many skills are built up in this gradual way.

And while you're dancing, how about teaching your dog to come to you and get up close? Tell him, 'Come', positioning your hands level with his nose. If you have a miniature dachshund, this will be at calf level; a Newfoundland, probably chest level. Hold a reward in your hand and wait until he has brought his body tightly up against yours. After doing this, he should, ideally, sit pressed up against you, his chin flat on your body, looking up at you.

Before we move on to the next session, let's consider the 'present' position, which is what we've just described, and then the 'finish' position. In the first, your dog is smack up in front of you, facing you and looking up. An expert trainer will have taught her dog to rest his head vertically against her legs (or body, depending on his height) so that he is looking directly up into her eyes. And so can you. When you call your dog to you, bribe him into position. Slowly you'll be able to bring him closer and closer in. Then, from the 'present' position, guide him from in front of you to around one side of you, then behind you (you may have to swap your reward from your right hand to your left), then to your left or right side – whichever side you've previously selected for lead and heelwork. Reward him.

As both you and your dog get used to this positioning, you'll end by asking him to sit cosily up against your chosen leg, with both of you facing in the same direction. The whole sequence from the 'present' position to the sit is called the 'finish' exercise. At first you may find it tricky to get your dog to sit square against your leg at the end of the exercise, but take it slowly and reward his efforts along the way.

I'll end this session with a great trick, but a tough one. Although I've trained only about six dogs to do this, you may be able to teach your dog to raise a back leg. In each of the six cases the owner did just as we've been doing here – waiting for the movement to occur (and, of course, I don't mean when he's urinating). As soon as he lifts one of his back legs off the ground (decide which one you prefer), no matter how small the movement, treat him. This is a perfect situation for using a clicker, as this tool helps you to quickly define a movement. If you're quick off the mark, you'll be able to click the second your dog has lifted or even slightly moved his leg, giving him a big hint that this movement is what won him the click and then the treat.

By the way, the six people whose dogs I trained to do this particular trick took months to perfect it. Give it a try, and if you've mastered it, please let me know, as I'd like to congratulate you personally.

Session 7: Rejection – who needs it?

You do. Rejection activities are very useful indeed and include requests such as 'no', 'give', 'leave', 'drop', 'off' and several more.

We think our dogs understand 'no'. But I can tell you that a great many of them haven't learned what it means, even though they hear the word all the time. Many dogs might even think it's their name, it's so often directed at them. If you're having problems with your dog *listening* to you when you say 'no', then I wager he doesn't know what you're asking of him. Luckily, you can remedy this situation pretty quickly.

If you have a novice dog, start by holding a treat in your hand and, after offering him a few opportunities to take it, use a moderate 'no' and withdraw your hand. Repeat this several times. Soon you'll begin to see your dog hesitate as he gets the hang of this game, which is just what you're aiming for. He's looking to you for instruction. Is it OK for me to have that treat? No? He's already begun to learn that there is a difference, whereas before, the word was meaningless to him.

Next place a treat on the ground and let your dog come to it and eat it. Do this several times. Then place another morsel on the ground, tell him 'no' and as he is heading towards it, pick it up so that he doesn't have a chance to get it. I know he'll look crushed, but it's for his own good, as well as yours. Repeat this several times. When he gets the hang of this little game, he won't go automatically to the treat but will listen first for your instructions. When he stays put, he has begun to understand the meaning of 'no'. Reward him.

Later, when you've learned how to give your dog a physical correction (see Corrections, p. 129), you'll be able to apply the use of 'no' as a warning – which may be necessary for some dogs. For instance, if your dog is making for the bin to put his head in it, you can tell him 'no' to warn him. If he doesn't heed your request, follow up with a correction. Most of the time he'll take your advice, and he may be grateful that you gave him a warning first.

The same method can be applied to teaching your dog not to pick up undesirable objects. If he is a bit of a rubbish collector, vacuuming up every dirty tissue and sweet wrapper as you walk along the street together, then teaching him to leave something alone is very handy indeed. Using 'no' is perfectly suitable here and in similar cases, but why not expand your dog's vocabulary?

To teach 'leave', place a ball, for instance, on the ground and allow your dog to pick it up and play with it. Do this a few times. When you no longer want him to pick it up, tell him 'leave' as he approaches it and make sure he can't get hold of it. Then you can give it to him, as you really don't need it, do you? (You can also teach him to leave something by adding a negative stimulus, like training discs or a rattling can, but please wait until we've covered this later on.) Try the exercise with increasingly tempting objects, but I warn you, you must be quick in grabbing back or covering the object, otherwise, if he 'wins' it, he'll think it's a game. You can also try to bribe your dog away from temptation. You know him best, so experiment to find what works well for the two of you.

The more your dog likes to pick things up off the ground or steal your (or other) children's toys, the more you'll need to work on this exercise. Persist, because it's a worthwhile instruction to teach him. I hope it's clear by now that our Hand Feeding routine is not only useful for encouraging your dog to do something good, but is also vital for steering him away from doing something undesirable.

Another rejection exercise is 'give' or 'drop' – whichever name you prefer. This is handy for whenever your dog has something in his mouth that you want him to relinquish. Let's say he loves to play with a ball, runs after it and kindly brings it back to you, but won't let go of it. After all, what's in it for him? However, because he is highly food-motivated by now, you can offer him something better than the ball: a delicious treat. Make sure that it is something exceptionally tasty, as an adrenalin-fuelled, ball-mad pooch is going to need a lot of tempting to give that ball up. I find dried liver treats work very well. When he does drop the ball, treat him handsomely. Then repeat the exercise if you wish, but don't wear out the ball routine. Some dogs like it less than others and you don't want to put yours off ball games. Eventually, after lots of practice and his having understood the movement and eventually the word 'give', you'll be able to let up on the titbits and reward him at the end of the game instead of all the way through.

But when, you ask, will we be showing you how to stop your dog terrorising pigeons on the street or diving into bushes after squirrels? Soon, very soon!

Session 8: Lazybones activities

Yes, this is exactly what it sounds like. You're going to be rewarding your dog for doing absolutely nothing at all. At least that's what he'll be thinking. In fact, you'll be teaching him activities such as 'wait' (or 'stay'), to ignore mild temptations, to walk carefully (or 'steady') and to stop (or 'still' or 'freeze', as you prefer).

I like to teach 'stay' in the same way as you've learned everything else here, by starting at the elementary level and waiting for the activity to happen. But then I like to see a stay varied and reinforced, so that it happens whatever the situation. It's a two-part approach.

Begin by waiting for your dog to be settled somewhere, like lying in front of the TV watching his favourite animal programme. Go up to him, tell him, 'Stay' and treat and praise him right there. Wow, treats for nothing. What a great surprise. You've just delivered part of his daily ration and at the same time you've escalated yourself to a new height of wonderfulness in his eyes. Do this any time you catch him doing nothing, just standing, lying or sitting still.

Now try to imitate this exercise by getting his attention and Hand Feeding him for staying still for a few moments, then for longer. After that, take a half-step backward, then a full step, then two and so on. Don't call your dog to you, but go back to him to reward him, otherwise you're rewarding him for coming to you, not for staying.

This is also a good time to introduce the request 'steady', which is simply a word to tell your dog to take it slow and easy. Use this when your dog is trying to be extra careful when doing something for the first time, like plank walking. Whenever he takes extra precautions, reward him with a titbit and finally add the word 'steady'. I find this very useful when my tribe get overexcited and I need them to take their energy level down a notch, or when I need to take a deep breath myself. Don't forget to treat your dog every step of the way.

You can also teach your dog to remain perfectly still, or 'freeze', so that he can be inspected, brushed or given medication. You can also teach him to balance a biscuit on his nose, or to hold an object, like his lead, in his mouth. For me, one of the most outstanding achievements is that none of my hand-fed trainees acts in a possessive manner or is protective about food. In practising 'still' and 'hold' exercises, your dog gets used to your hand being on him and in his mouth. It becomes the greatest thing in his life and the more he has of it the better.

So, to begin, settle your dog down next to you. Relax him by giving him a gentle tummy scratch, or whatever he finds pleasing and calming. When he is relaxed and still, withdraw your hand and reward him. Repeat the relaxation part, varying what you do, until he has begun to associate having your hands placed on him without himself moving. For instance, you can place a finger lightly on the top of his head, or your whole hand under his chin. Ask him to be still. If he is still for a second, treat him and tell him he's a good boy. Really strive for perfection, as doing it properly for just a second is much more valuable than a minute of a less successful 'still'. 'Still' needs to be just that: no movement whatsoever.

Beagle Leia demonstrates a proper 'hold'. A rose by any other name...

Gradually become more demanding, asking him to be still for longer periods of time – but take care to progress at a snail's pace. If he moves he misses out on his reward, and you'll need to start again. Start with one or two seconds, and slowly build from there. If you can get him up to a minute one day, you'll have joined the ranks of the professionals.

Now start moving your hands around his face, but don't overdo it. You'll know when you've gone too far. You can probably overpower your dog at this stage, but remember, the whole purpose of our training is to gain his cooperation. Don't use force, just gently rest your hands wherever you wish and let him develop your trust.

Gradually work with your dog to relax his head so that you can move it slightly up and down, left and right. This is harder than you think, as at first he'll try to resist you. Take it slowly, with tiny movements and short time intervals, and generously praise every success, however small. As your dog feels comfortable, you should also be able to play with his ears, look into his eyes and handle his paws so that you can inspect between his toes. Why? Because your dog needs to be comfortable and content with being handled. You can't let him get away with being handled only on his terms – it has to be an agreement between the two of you. Practising all of this will also be particularly useful when you take him to the vet or groomer.

You may be wondering why we target a dog's head in this exercise. The head has, in fact, more nerve endings and sensitive zones than anywhere else on his outer body. With very sensitive dogs, you may wish to start with the back or neck, eventually moving up to the head and so achieving total trust and control.

One of the biggest steps you'll ever be able to take in building your dog's repertoire of obedience will be to get him to retrieve all sorts of objects. The 'still' is an invaluable foundation for this skill. It is well worth practising and has many happy side effects, including the establishment of trust, tolerance, acceptance, loyalty and manageability.

You can add a bit of creativity to the 'still' routine by placing things in his mouth and then asking him to stay still. But make sure it's nothing bad-tasting, like a lemon or a plastic bag, or unsafe, like a coin. Use your common sense and be sensitive to your dog. Once you've placed the object in his mouth and asked him to be still, praise and treat him (or click and treat) even if he does it for only a couple of seconds. Gradually build up to longer times.

Have you seen dogs doing product endorsements in TV commercials, leaving their paws on top of an object? This is all accomplished with exercises similar to the 'still' game and is easily learned through the above technique. Other exercises that you can teach at this time and in this way are 'take it', 'bring it', 'swap' and 'give'.

Session 9: Obstacle training

Jake, a handsome Newfoundland, loves obstacle and article training and often does display shows for charity.

With all the knowledge you now have, you'll be able to teach your dog a variety of moves involving obstacles. These skills include getting up on to things and off again, getting in and out of cars, jumping through hula hoops, walking up and down A-frames, walking across planks, tunnelling, weaving around poles or through your legs, walking on a seesaw, hurtling over jumps, staying on contact boxes and walking carefully. Some of these obstacles are, of course, used in agility training, but it's no problem if you don't have this professional equipment. If you're going to be teaching your dog these exercises for fun rather than for the purposes of competition, you can learn the basics and apply them to suitable obstacles you may find in your home or outdoors. The important thing here is to experiment and create your own challenges for yourself and your dog.

However, if you prefer to practise on professional equipment, the best way is to join an agility club. There you'll have hands-on professionals to help you through the course and prepare you for competitions, if that's what you and your dog wish to do.

In Session 5 one of the things you learned was the basics of jumping. So why not try teaching your dog how to step over, and eventually jump over, a brick, plank, book, ball, or a few items for a long jump? You can also teach your dog to jump up on to something and jump off. A lot of people like to practise this at home. Would you like your dog to join you on the sofa? Invite him by telling him, 'Up'. Offer him a treat on your lap. If he's just putting his front paws up, treat him for that and build up to getting his whole body on to the sofa.

You can do this by placing the treat towards you and the back of the sofa, guiding him to lean further in towards you. Eventually he'll have to get himself up there if he wants that titbit. Take it one paw at a time, slowly and gradually as always. When you want him to get off the sofa, put a treat on the floor and say, 'Down' (or 'Off'). This exercise is also useful for getting your dog on to and off the table at the vet's, which can be difficult, especially if he's a big dog that is too heavy to pick up. (If you're concerned about your dog getting on the sofa without permission, my and many trainers' response is to put the behaviour on a cue in order to rid him of it. If your dog isn't asked to do something, he just may not do it!)

Indy flies over a jump.

Now how about teaching him to get in and out of the back of the car, or in and out of his bath? The same principles apply as for 'up' and 'down'. You encourage your dog into the car with a treat, rewarding the small movements he makes in the right direction. If you have a dog that is particularly reluctant to try this little adventure, put a sturdy and safely positioned box just in front of the boot to give him an extra step. Encourage him up, first, on that. Once this is accomplished, you can teach him to get out of the car, offering him a reward when he does. Again, you may need to use an intermediate step at first, to make it easier for him to jump down.

If you're still having trouble mastering these jumps, you're certainly not up to scratch with the basic exercise where your dog follows your hand with food in it (see p. 86). Go back and just Hand Feed him for 'left', 'right', 'this way' and 'back', 'twirl' and 'over', into the car. Going back to kindergarten for a while will save you time in the long run and help you move forward once more.

If you want to train your dog to jump through a hula hoop, or just your arms, it's simply a matter of starting at a low level and building him up to greater heights. In the case of the hula hoop, stand it upright on the ground, supporting it with one hand, and encourage him to jump through it by offering a reward. As he grows more and more confident, raise the hoop gradually higher.

Be sensitive to your dog's capabilities. Some can jump higher than others; it's just a matter of figuring out what height yours is happy with. Use two or three hoops for a long jump, but bear in mind that some dogs are naturally well coordinated, while some are not. The clumsy ones' coordination can be developed and improved, however. You just have to start with smaller jumps and advance more slowly.

With hurdles, start at a low level and work your way up. Another approach to jumping hurdles is to do it yourself, to encourage him to imitate your actions.

Often when I'm on Hampstead Heath, walking through the woods with my canine buddies, we find a nice thick fallen tree on which to practise our plank walking exercise. I encourage them to get on to the tree and walk along it. For novice owners and dogs, the big challenge can be just getting the dog up there, so we have to start working on that first, taking baby steps as described for 'up' and 'off'. Once a dog is on the tree, I encourage him, one paw at a time, to walk along it. With this accomplished, you and your dog have learned the basics of plank walking and can make the challenges harder if you wish. For instance, try to get him to jump over your back as you lie face down or kneel on all fours on the ground. It's a great game!

You can train your dog to jump over obstacles, like fallen trees, or use professional agility equipment as seen here.

In agility, tunnels are used as part of the obstacle course. Collapsible ones allow you to alter the length of the tunnel. Start with it fairly short. You can either guide your dog through with a treat or throw this into the tunnel to encourage him to venture inside. Some dogs feel a bit anxious or even noticeably claustrophobic about doing this, so it's important you don't rush this exercise. Let your dog get used to approaching the tunnel and placing a paw in it. Then ask for two paws, then the whole body, until finally, after much practice, you're able to encourage him to go right through the tunnel. Whatever you do, don't physically push him. He'll distrust the whole process, and perhaps you – the opposite of what you want to achieve. As your dog grows more confident, you can start attaching a word to this game, like 'tunnel' or 'through', 'in' or 'under'.

Another obstacle is the weaving poles, which are simply tall, narrow stakes that are equally spaced in a line in the ground for the dogs to weave around. One of the simplest ways to teach your dog to do this is to use purpose-made walls or fences that narrow down the options of where he can go. However, the 'weave' can just as easily be taught by guiding your dog through the poles with a reward. Take it slowly at first and eventually you'll be able to increase your speed. You may also wish to teach this exercise by holding a stick at the far end of the poles to serve as a target.

Dima and Cuba demonstrate how to weave.

A further application of the 'weave' is using your own legs as the obstacle. Begin first by standing still. Start with your dog on your left side and move your right foot forward. Using your right hand, tame your dog with a treat held between your legs so that he comes out on to your right side and around the treat. Reward him. Now move your left foot forward and, with your left hand, guide him between your legs so that he ends up by your left side. Reward and repeat. Build this exercise up so that eventually you'll be able to walk fairly naturally and your dog will run from one side to the next. Note that this is an exercise that is harder to execute, if not impossible, with really large dogs, simply because they are too tall to go under most people's legs.

The A-frame is just that: a wide frame in the shape of the letter A. The great thing about it is that it is adjustable, so you can start your dog on one that is nearly flat, encouraging him one paw at a time as he walks from one end, over the top of the A and down the other side. Bit by bit, as his skill improves, you can use sharper inclines.

In agility training there is also a contact box or table that a dog has to jump up on to and stay on. The training for this is the same for training your dog to stay in one spot, as well as to go to any object and to stay there (see Distance control commands, p. 124).

Ciao, baby

You've done well. You'd like a little quiet time for yourself and to let your dog do his own thing for the moment, I'm sure. Well, how are you going to tell him that? You could ignore him, of course, but is there another way? Yes, you can tell him. You're quickly learning how to communicate with your dog, so why not let him know when he can go off and play on his own? The reason for teaching this is simply that dogs need to know how much they are supposed to work. We interrupt all training almost every 10–15 minutes, even more often in the beginning, with some playtime. It helps refresh those tense zones in their inexperienced minds and stimulates their bodies too.

I like the expressions 'go play', 'free' or 'off you go'. Let's say you're in the park, you've done lots of moves and it's time to just walk and relax. Throw a fist full of titbits on to the ground and tell him, 'Go play', allowing him to go and collect them. Close your treat bag and keep it closed until you want to call him for any reason. Just as with any of the other moves and words he has learned, after enough consistent practice he'll understand what you're requesting.

He'll appreciate having a break, to finally have that toy he's been thinking about, or to stretch his legs and chase some scavenging birds – as long as the activity is safe and authorised by you.

All dogs need a chance to play and refresh their minds.
Co-co has a game of ball.

Session 10: Distance control commands

One of the most advanced and therefore important skills needed if you are to be in full control of your dog is distance control: being able to deliver commands to him at a distance and get him to comply. How many things can your dog do at about 30 feet away from you? What about 70 or 100 feet? How do you gain control when your dog is on the other side of a field somewhere? It isn't enough that he may choose to come back eventually. It is vital that he return on your command, and this is where distance control training comes into play.

Most untrained dogs don't even know what we look like from a distance, never mind what 'stay' or 'stop it' means. Therefore you'll have to master the same tricks and moves you learned earlier, 'sit', 'stay', 'stand', 'down' and so on, only at greater and greater distances. You'll start from only a few feet away from your dog, and you'll work hard to help him learn each move correctly. Furthermore, all dogs are different, so you may have to try a few things to see what works best for the two of you.

Solution 1. From only a few steps away, tell your dog, 'Down', then try to stretch forward and deliver a titbit right by his front legs, encouraging him to comply. After a few repetitions he'll start to anticipate this move and will lie down where he is instead of coming to you. Gradually build up the distance between you.

Solution 2. Another way to teach your dog distance control is to tie his lead to a stationary object, like a radiator, or, if outside, a fence, tree or helpful friend, stand some distance away and ask him to lie down, giving him a bit of time to do so. Cut down the distance if you feel it will make it easier for your dog. If he has cooperated with you earlier, this challenge won't be such hard work for him. Increase the distance only when he has mastered the current one.

Repeat this exercise for 'sit-ups' and 'stand-ups', using a clicker if you wish, and improve the variety of training situations. This will keep you busy for a few days.

Another distant control command that I like to teach is 'Go to bed'. No, I'm not asking dogs to go and snuggle up in their owner's comfy bed – most of them have that luxury anyway. No, it's just a phrase that can be used for any object you want your dog to go to and settle down on. It can be a lead, sweater, blanket, or even a set of keys or a mobile phone, as well as a bed, of course – anything handy. This is pretty much the same as obedience competition trainers teach in the 'send away' command.

At first, get your dog to pick up a few treats from the ground, and begin to increase your distance after you've dropped them. Then place your designated object on the ground and bribe your dog to come to it. When he reaches the object, treat him. Easy enough so far. Place the object a couple of feet away and now, when your dog is looking, place a treat on the object and say, 'Go to bed' as he rushes over for his reward. This is a hard exercise, so take it slowly. I shouldn't try anything more adventurous the first time. Instead, break the exercise into three steps. Don't progress from one step to the next until your dog shows enough confidence in what he's supposed to be doing. Then you can teach him to run to it from longer distances, then to look for the 'bed' both in and out of your sight.

Coleman makes a splash.

The next time you are looking for something to train in him, you can begin to get your dog to lie down, settle or sit by the object (or 'mark') in the three steps. You may no longer have to throw the treat to the object as a bribe, as he will go to it eventually automatically. Let him go to his mark, and when he reaches it, give him his reward. Then ask him to lie down and reward him once more. The third and final step is to get him to go to his mark and lie down automatically without any intervention from you. When he has accomplished this consistently over time, you won't have to treat him every step of the way, but only occasionally and at the end of the whole process. If you find he's not doing it properly, go back to the level where he is confident and build up again from there.

Before you go off to practise, I'll explain where you can go from here. You may teach your dog to perform many tasks without being close by, and many of the tricks are used in the modelling and film jobs our dogs do from time to time. Working on set and posing dogs for the camera without any help or guidance is a big part of any casting project. Often dogs have to do a 'high five', 'hold', 'paw', 'bow', 'lie flat' or one of the many other moves that we've already introduced. So, as a step up in your training, why not try to make all your dog's moves work from a few feet away, then further and further? Whether your dog is destined for the screen or not, you'll most likely need to use distance control for many real-life situations. The absolute musts are: distance (emergency) stays, instant recalls from far away, 'no' at any distance and, of course, 'sit' and 'down'.

These emergency control commands have often, in my experience, saved a dog's life. Many people feel that, once they are taught these skills, they are the very best they have learned from the Good Boy Dog School. You can never overdo your training for these exercises, as there is no such thing as a too-well-behaved dog.

Congratulations! You've not only learned the basics of obedience training, but have advanced to a level many dogs and their owners have never even dreamed of reaching. Go and celebrate, but meet me back here when you're ready, as I have several more challenges and finishing touches in store for the two of you.

Hand Feeding by others

There is no reason why you shouldn't enlist others, if they're willing, to help you in training your dog. Strangers, friends, workmen, even the postman, can Hand Feed him so that he develops a liking for people. His singular intention, when seeing people, will be to run up to them to see if they have any food for him. If they don't, they'll be uninteresting and he'll leave them in peace. If they do have treats, don't be surprised to see him go through a variety of show-stopping moves to win them over. In this way he will see people as the opportunity to learn, succeed and win, and this mental and physical stimulation is an integral part of the Hand Feeding routine.

None of the dogs that have gone through our Hand Feeding programme growls, protects or attacks humans. Whatever would they do that for? They get goodies and make lots of friends because they have learned how to be well mannered and are keen to learn. They've got doga-tude. They know that the world is a wonderful place filled with good things, when they act pleasingly. They understand there's nothing to gain by behaving otherwise.

Hand Feeding is a great way for everyone to participate in your dog's training programme. Our illustrator, Nika, shows us how it's done.

Weaning your dog off titbits

There comes a time when you won't want to treat your dog after every single compliance. Instead, you'll want to vary your pattern of rewarding and make it unpredictable. By now your dog understands all your requests but you no longer have to keep up the regular 'payments'.

Let's say you've asked your dog to come to heel by your side. You may be treating him every ten paces or so, maybe more. Now, you can mix it up. Deliver a reward after five, then 30, then 40, then ten paces.

Or let's say you're asking your dog to do a routine of moves, like 'distance down', 'come', 'present' and 'finish'. You can choose to treat him once or twice during this routine, just once at the end, or even at the beginning. The key is not to be predictable. In this way your dog will never know when his reward will come (though he knows it will), so he'll be keen to do everything you ask in anticipation of his much-wanted treat.

There are many regimes that you can employ to cut down on the quantity of rewards, but don't surrender the idea of what we call 'playing positively'. All living things need encouragement to develop and flourish. Vary the ratio of exercises to rewards, the interval between training sessions and the duration of sessions, as this will achieve unpredictability, thereby keeping your dog's attention. Continue to mix up these three variables and you'll constantly progress. One day you won't even have to think about such tactics: they'll just come naturally because of both the expertise you have acquired and your dog's understanding of what you expect of him in training.

Corrections

You may feel that although things are going very well for you and your dog, there is still something missing. Indeed, there is. The training you've just completed is appropriate for most of the challenges your dog will face. He is likely to be behaving – until he has to decide between you and doing doggie things, like swimming in a pond. And then the pond wins most times. Sound familiar?

So, with some dogs in some limited situations, this is the point where you'll need to introduce corrections into your training. This is the finishing touch and is based on what is individually appropriate for each dog. Before you wince at the mere thought of it, let me inform you that dogs appreciate being told that what they are doing isn't right. When they are pups their mothers tell them off by snarling at them, pushing them aside, giving them a little nip and so on. Also, older dogs give the very clear signal of bared teeth, often accompanied by a snarl and a snap, to a younger dog when he is misbehaving or being too rambunctious. There are countless situations where dogs send each other negative messages to communicate their thoughts and position in the hierarchy.

So it is perfectly natural for you too, as your dog's guide and leader, to deliver corrections when required. The aim in this final stage is to brush up your training by combining what is nice for your dog to do for rewards with an explanation of what he shouldn't do. These elements must occur together, not singly.

In using corrections we teach a dog about what we don't want him to do by delivering an unpleasant consequence. But, in doing so, we aren't successfully informing him as to what we do want him to do. If we're only talking about a single misbehaviour, without which the dog is 100% reliable, a single reprimand of moderate strength may prove extremely efficient. In my experience, though, it's never the case that a misbehaving dog has only one problem area. Dogs normally have quite a range of bad habits and therefore introducing a reprimand to correct one will push them further away from us rather than helping to resolve the difficulty. (See Chapter 9 for advice on common behavioural problems.)

If you still have reservations about it, think about the 'Hot and Cold' game. As I'm writing these lines, I've invited my elder son, Nick, to participate in a little experiment to illustrate my point about the helpfulness of corrections. I've silently chosen a miniature object on my shelf, and his job is to figure out what I've selected as I navigate him towards it. However, in a deviation from the game, I've only told him he is 'hot' when he is closing in. I never tell him he's 'cold' when he is digressing. It takes Nick three minutes to find my chosen object.

Then we try the game conventionally, using both 'hot' and 'cold'. This time it takes him only 17 seconds. Amazing, isn't it? And all because we also used negative messaging, the acknowledgement of failure. I don't know why so many people think of a negative stimulus as a punishment; it doesn't have to be. How upset do you think Nick was when I indicated he was moving in the wrong direction? I think he was, in fact, relieved, as the 'cold' message made my communication clearer and therefore his task easier. He was looking for any message from me that would help him to succeed. In effect, he was depending on me as his team mate.

It is the same with communicating with your dog. It can sometimes make it easier for him to understand what you're trying to tell him if he is given guidance of a negative nature by someone he trusts and knows is on his side.

At some of my workshops I demonstrate the use of a 'magic' touch as a way of reprimanding a dog. Each time a dog responds to a command in the wrong way, I just walk up to him and touch him with an index finger. This comes as a surprise to the spectators as much as it does to the animal. Having had so many rewards and then suddenly no reward, plus that odd touch, he'd be left confused, you'd think. But the difference to him is clear and obvious. Most importantly, there's no need to go much further than that – at least not with dogs that think positively and are keen to get it right – and this is another reason to concentrate on the positive side of training and Hand Feed them with good habits.

Experts in canine behaviour have come up with other effective ways to achieve such communication. John Rogerson employs a plastic bottle with some dried pasta inside that he shakes or drops on the ground; Roger Mugford throws an aluminium drink can a quarter to a third filled with pebbles or dry pasta; John Fisher prefers his training discs; Gary Wilkes hurls a wet cloth or towel; some use ultrasonic devices, others an Abeistop (a citronella-filled collar) or a metal choke chain, throwing it as a noise-making tool. At our school we've even used Beanie Babies, little and light, to illustrate the need for timing and consistency and to indicate 'yes' and 'no' in the dog-training version of Hot and Cold. But this can only work on the condition that your dog and you are playing on the same side, a relationship that can be nurtured by our Hand Feeding routine.

So what should you use to correct your dog? Before you start working with him again, give him a bit of rest while you do some homework. Divide a large piece of paper into two halves. On the left side, head it 'Ten Things My Dog Loves'; on the right side, 'Ten Things My Dog Hates'. On the left, jot down everything your dog thinks is wonderful in life, and on the right, the best examples of what he simply hates. Try to write down a minimum of ten things in each list, although I bet you can come up with far more. Your list may look something like this:

TEN THINGS MY DOG LOVES (Positive reinforcers)	TEN THINGS MY DOG HATES (Negative stimuli)
Sleeping on the sofa/bed	Being pushed off the sofa/bed
Getting scraps from the table	Being ignored at the dinner table
Playing fetch	The noise of the vacuum cleaner
Liver treats	Being smacked with a newspaper*
Chicken	Seeing carrots fed to the rabbit
Squeaky toys	Being ignored
Raw hide	Being put back on a lead
Rough play	Loud noises
Having his belly scratched	Training discs
Riding in the car	Having water sprayed at him

* Inhumane but a popular disciplinary tool in the past

Many, but by no means all, of the list on the left can be used in the appropriate manner as reinforcers in your training. Looking at the list on the right, you'll see that some of your dog's dislikes are of your own making, through neglect. Take the vacuum cleaner, for instance. Many dogs don't like this because they weren't introduced to it properly and remain frightened of it. The use of a vacuum isn't an appropriate disciplinary tool, for we aren't interested in instilling any negative feelings, however slight, in your dog to correct his misbehaviour. (Not to mention the obvious fact that it would be difficult to take a vacuum cleaner out with you everywhere you go and to start it up every time your dog tries to jump on a passer-by on the street.) We only want to *inform* him.

However, if your dog is lying on the sofa with you, watching his favourite *National Geographic* re-run on the migration of Canada geese and begins to bark, one example of an appropriate reprimand would be to chuck him off your lap and on to the floor, and not let him back up. If your dog is whining at you or playing up in any way while you're eating dinner, suitable responses would be to ignore him completely, shut him in another room, or put him in a travel kennel and give him a chew toy the moment he settles down.

You know what your dog enjoys and what he doesn't, and so you're best able to come up with creative reward and aversion techniques to train him. But beware of the 'ignoring your dog' routine – touted in some popular training books as a cure-all – as it's not about what you do, but how you leave your dog thinking about his actions, that actually counts. When he picks up a fried chicken wing off the pavement, turning your back on him is probably not the best idea, as isn't that what he's really hoping you'll do? Ignoring, if properly administered, means that the positive stimulus is completely terminated, with no chance for alternative fun. Can you always do it? Of course not: it's just not practical.

When making your 'negative' list, try to leave out as well those superficial incidents like him not letting you have a cigarette (might be worth listening to that one, though!) or pick up another dog as it makes him jealous. We can't consistently use these and others. We want to change your dog's attitude to these issues, not use them as motivators. Take your pen and circle the items you've listed that you feel can be employed practically and which will get your dog to think about his actions. Then get someone else to look at them for you and see if they agree. These will be the items to employ.

On the positive side of your list, there may be other things besides treats that will act as positive reinforcements, helping your dog to understand what is required of him. Try the exercises below to begin thinking about what will work best for him. You'll see that you have many alternatives at your disposal, all of which are harmless but moderate enough to be effective.

The use of corrections depends on your dog. You'll need to evaluate the *frequency* of his bad behaviour; its (*intensity*); how long it lasts (*duration*); in what context it occurs; and its meaning (*sense*). Examining these factors will help you to shape a programme of corrections. You may be lucky enough to need to correct your dog only occasionally for just one type of bad behaviour, or you may have a dog with multiple problem areas, each of which requires you to give him frequent instruction. Consider his issue(s) carefully. This will help you decide on how best to correct him.

Also, when considering corrections, be aware that sometimes the behaviour you're trying to stop or prevent will result in some other unruly manifestation because your dog's adrenalin is running high. And for this reason his new behaviour can be much worse. So, first teach your dog the acceptable alternative to his behaviour, anticipate possible manifestations, and when you're ready both mentally and physically, give it a try. You shouldn't tolerate a dog that pulls down the microwave just because you've contained him in the kitchen, or sinks his teeth into your leg just because you drag him away to stop him attacking your neighbour. But how to begin?

Nellie, a Cavalier King Charles Spaniel.

To get you started, let's run through some of the most successfully used physical tools for communicating a negative message to your dog in order to achieve a positive result. The following exercises will help you decide what will work most effectively for your dog.

Correction exercise 1: the tap

One way to correct your dog is to give him a reminding tap with your finger. I usually aim for a dog's shoulder blade, or if his backside is closer, his rump. The tap shouldn't be hard. How hard? I recommend no more than what it would take to push an egg without breaking its shell. It's just as if you're tapping someone on the shoulder to ask for directions. As in the use of a check, the tap is a form of instruction. It's a way of telling your dog, 'Sorry, that's not quite right – think again' or, 'Look to me for guidance.'

Although for the exercise below I advise you to put your dog on the lead, you'll be able to use the tap in any circumstance where your dog is close enough for you to reach him. Get some treats ready and put your dog on the lead. You can do this exercise inside or outside. Ask your dog to sit. Throw the treats out in front of him, a couple of feet away, so they are slightly out of his reach. Naturally, he'll go towards them, extending himself to the end of his lead. As he does so, give him a tap. When you've done this exercise a few times, he will remain sitting in order to avoid the tap and to win instead a treat for doing as he was originally asked to do: to sit.

Similarly, if your dog is begging at the table and you want him to stop, you can tell him by delivering a tap.

Correction exercise 2: the water spray

Another handy corrective device is water. Those who know me, humans and canines alike, are familiar with my trusty ketchup bottle. I always have it filled and at the ready at home, and I often take it with me when training misbehaving dogs. You can also use a spray bottle, like the ones you use to water plants. It's a simple tool to use. (If you're recycling a bottle, make sure that it's completely clean and free of chemicals, as you may spray your dog in the face and you don't want the water to affect him in any other way.)

Ask your dog to stay. Use a tennis ball or another object that he finds particularly tempting, and toss it near him. If he stays put, reward him with a treat, or click and treat. If he doesn't stay, give him a short burst of water.

You may even consider using a super-cool, space-wars kind of water gun. I sometimes see people employing these in the park, and although it may be, rather perversely, fun to use, I don't wish to carry around a huge, indiscreet weapon. You want something that gently sprays water, not pumps it out like a firefighter's hose. It should be a tool that is easy to use and to time, and one that you can deploy quickly and from a short distance.

Correction exercise 3: the check

Begin by walking your dog from one point to another as you normally would in the house or somewhere where he behaves consistently well. No problems, right? Now try doing this in a situation where you know he will *not* act 100% correctly – that is, heeling by your side when you're walking past a group of dogs, children with toys or a garden with squirrels. However, it's better to start with milder distractions.

When walking outside, keep your dog on the lead. Have a biscuit in your hand and get him to follow this treat. The moment he looks away, having been distracted by other stimuli, check him lightly with the lead. When he begins to pay attention to you and the titbit, reward him for doing so, as this is what you want him to do. Then repeat the process again and again, delivering a check when required, and handing out lots of rewards as he follows and looks to you. A check with the lead is undesirable to your dog and is the mildest way to correct him. If you let him off the lead after a few successes so that he can go and have a little game, this will work as a perfect positive reinforcer.

How do you determine the strength of the check? It doesn't have to be any more than what it would take for someone to tug your shirt while you're writing and to have your penmanship skewed. But remember, this will work only if the lead is slack and comfortable at all other times. So, no tight lead – slack, slack, *SLACK!*

But there are other ways to caution your dog if a check on the lead, a spray of water or a gentle tap is inappropriate for the particular moment. For instance, if your dog is at home with you and not on the lead, it's impossible to deliver a check with it. Let's look at what you can do then.

Other corrective tools

All of the above are moderate, harmless ways to correct your dog's intentional or unintentional mistakes. Training discs, found in most pet shops, also fall into this category and can be used as a viable alternative. Developed by John Fisher, these are simply thrown on the ground – but eventually just rattled in your hand – when you want to correct your dog's behaviour. If you've asked him to sit but he then lunges for the treats or ball you've thrown on the ground as a distraction, you can toss the discs to alert him to his error. Training discs are a personal favourite of mine because they are easy to carry and have at the ready. Since timing is crucial in correcting your dog, discs are a very efficient tool.

Dr Mugford's drink can containing pebbles and with the open end sealed with tape is an excellent little noise-maker similar in effect to training discs. Or you can fill up a plastic bottle with pebbles. Knocking it against your thigh might also do the trick, in which case there's the bonus that you don't have to pick it up afterwards.

The choke chain (or Woodhouse chain, after its great advocate Barbara Woodhouse) is another useful device. But, unlike the way she used it, I recommend you toss it on the ground to make a noise that will help you to correct your dog. Like training discs, it is very lightweight and handy.

The command 'no' isn't initially a negative stimulus and so it can only be used as a correction as a signal that has been conditioned within a negative sequence. As Gary Wilkes says in his *Behavior Sampler*, it is only logical to use 'no' before delivering a correction, not during or after. The whole point of doing this is that you may not have to reprimand a dog that has taken your advice and cooperates:

> ...imagine that I have a broom, and the nasty habit of sneaking up from behind and whacking you with it. If you require me to say the word 'duck,' would you want me to say it before I hit you, as I hit you, or after I hit you? If you decide to have me yell 'duck' before I hit you, you have made the right choice.

In this way your dog gets fair warning that if he doesn't cease his behaviour he'll receive some type of correction (but not a whack with a broom as in the above analogy!). When your dog learns that this is so – that you really mean no when you say it – he'll begin to hesitate and eventually stop doing what he was thinking about doing or had already started to do. He'll realise quickly that crime just doesn't pay! However, if you say 'no', your dog ignores this and you don't follow it up with a correction, he will understand that 'no' doesn't mean anything at all. You'll have taught him that there are no negative consequences for his actions, only continuous rewards.

Correcting when you aren't present

The occasional brainy canine may figure out early on that the cause of all his misfortune is you. When you are around, he gets in trouble. But when you go out to do your shopping he can have a grand old time opening the fridge, raiding the bin, sleeping on the furniture, overturning flower pots – all this without any interference from you. Clever dog!

You'll be pleased to know that you don't need to be a genius to outmanoeuvre your dog in this instance. All it takes is a good strategy to stand up to him, and there is a solution for every type of nuisance. You can use either of two approaches (or both together) to rid him of all his bad habits. The first is containment by means of a travel kennel or child guard to keep your dog away from the things you want him to leave alone – and in time he may forget his obsession with these things (this is discussed later in Management solutions, p. 192). The second is aversion: the use of a programmed corrective device that you activate when bad behaviour occurs.

Aversion strategy 1. Set up your chosen remote-controlled gadget – this will use spray, sound or another deterrent – and hook up a CCTV or video camera so that you can spy on your dog from outside the house as he is going about his job of search and destroy. As you watch him and he begins to pick up a shoe, investigate the kitchen counter, gnaw on a table leg or whatever, you can activate your device to issue a correction. He'll soon associate his bad behaviour with the bad stimuli and he'll quickly learn not to do it. His bad patterns will be broken; his bad behaviour eradicated. This is an expensive formula, but a very effective one.

Aversion strategy 2. An option for use when you aren't at home is a bit like the booby-trap in *Home Alone*, except it's you who is setting up the aversions. Earlier we looked at corrective tools like training discs and other noise-makers. Once you've introduced these to your dog and found them effective, you can use them while he is at home on his own.

Imagine your spoilt little pal likes to sneak into your study and rummage through your bin, leaving chewed-up bits of paper all over the floor like snowflakes. Now imagine that you've booby-trapped the door with a can filled with pebbles and when your bin destroyer pushes open the door, the can comes crashing down on the floor with a loud bang. Will he want to do this again? He's going to think twice, believe me, as his only mission in life is to enjoy himself. This awful noise is going to make him rethink what he is doing. Reset the booby-trap every time you go out and you'll know that when the study door stays closed, you've won the game.

West Highland White Terrier, Musetta

Aversion strategy 3. In the same vein, you can train your dog to not remove food or any other objects from their resting place when you aren't around. With a piece of string, tie a ladle, a cooking pan (not too heavy), training discs, or can of pebbles to a bit of safe, doggy-digestible human food and place it on the kitchen work surface. When Mr Sneaky tries to remove it, he's going to get a very nasty surprise – again a loud bang will mark his bad behaviour. Keep this up and it will make him reconsider his ambitions. You may need to experiment with various types of food and other items he likes to chew, like shoes, putting them in different places around the house. In this way you'll establish no-go zones.

Try to outplay a very clever dog by using different tools and a variety of traps. Keep things unpredictable. This is where training turns very individual – when you have to take into consideration your dog's sensitivities and your skills. But you've already learned that patience is an essential part of the training game. In addition, you have a real advantage: all the practice and time you've put into teaching your dog all that is good in this world will have convinced him that the two of you are playing on the same side. In his eyes you're both part of the same team, tribe and family.

Reprimanding your dog

The use of reprimand – aversion techniques, punishment, negative stimulation and telling off – in any form is a very sophisticated tool of the trade that in the right hands will do precisely what it is meant to, and no more. If used in the wrong hands, however, it will cause more harm than good. In some cases the damage may be irreversible. Besides, the section on Management solutions (p. 192) offers the owner of a troublesome dog many ways to coexist with the animal without having to resort to reprimand. Here I strongly recommend that you use the right tool for your particular problem, as this will save you aggravation and the need to administer punishment.

Don't look for short cuts or quick fixes for your dog's problems, using punishment just because you're too lazy to learn about the ways to avoid difficult situations or to try proven tools. If, after doing either or both, you're still looking for solutions, I'll tell you a better, easier and more reliable way to tackle your issues and to bring harmony in your human-dog relationship.

This said, there may be instances when you'll require something stronger than a light check, a tap or a throw of the training discs to inform your dog that what he is doing is wrong. I'd like to talk about the use of reprimand here, but not on a practical level, as I don't feel it is ethical to try to train anyone in this matter solely by means of a book. Instead, my focus is on its value in educating the misbehaving dog. Punishment, for that is what it is, is an uncomfortable topic for many people, mainly because we know that it so often has a detrimental effect on a dog. In fact, I'm not an opponent of the use of reprimand, and accept that it can be effective if done correctly. And if it is done correctly, it will need to be used just once, or extremely rarely, and even then probably in the mildest possible way.

However, it takes a very experienced, objective person and perfect timing to implement it properly. That's why, if it is to be used, it is important to have a qualified professional handler with years of experience to show you how to do it properly.

Reprimands should be used only to educate your dog that his behaviour isn't wanted, and not as a form of revenge. There is a fine line between punishment and abuse, and I'm afraid that many can't walk it without falling towards violence.

Pamela Reid is one of the current authorities on the subject and theory of reprimand. Her book *Excel-Erated Learning* is very clinical but gives a fascinating insight into the behaviour of dogs and the use of punishment to correct it.

Here is a summary of a few of her main points:

• If you plan to use aversive consequences as punishment, you have a responsibility to know exactly what you're doing so that you won't cause your dog any physical or psychological harm.
• A reprimand is most educational if it tells your dog what he is supposed to do as opposed to what he is not. Teaching an alternative behaviour by causing a happy consequence is extremely effective. For instance, if your dog likes to bark at cyclists, give him something else to do when you see a cyclist coming. Focus him on something positive, like asking him to sit and giving him a treat when he does. He can't sit and chase at the same time! This is what is called 'positive reinforcement' (see also p. 28).

• If punishment is to be used, it must be done immediately. Clinical tests prove that the closer the punishment is in time to the behaviour, the less likely it will be seen again in the future. An immediate reaction is vital. Anything else is less effective, and if enough time separates the behaviour and the consequence, the punishment will be absolutely meaningless to him – for instance, swatting your dog with a rolled-up newspaper after you've discovered a urine stain on the carpet hours later. The dog won't string together his eliminating on the carpet an hour ago and the punishment he has just received.

However, if the punishment is administered within two seconds of the misbehaviour, there is an almost 100% chance that the dog will remember the consequences. If it is done more than five seconds afterwards, the chance is less than 60% (this follows too in the case of rewards). Although experiments show that dogs have memory traces even after punishment followed a 30-minute delay, it's not worth risking use of an extreme measure for what will probably have little or no positive result. *So be quick, or be quiet!*

• You must be consistent in your use of punishment. If you squirt water at your dog *every time* he steals food from the kitchen, it will be much more effective than if you do it only every other time or every so often.

• The further removed you are personally from the use of the punishment, the less likely it is that *you* will be seen by your dog as a negative stimulus. Remote-activated devices such as citronella collars are more effective than using your hand. But they must only be used as professionally instructed. As we said earlier, items like training discs, a check on the lead, a spray of water or a choke chain are all effective correction tools.

You need to research carefully the strength, schedule and intensity of a negative reinforcement before equipping yourself with reprimand tools. So take a good look at the available information.

Furthermore, if your dog is exhibiting behaviour that you feel requires punishment, consult a professional before devising any kind of strategy. It is your responsibility to know exactly what you're doing for the sake of your dog. And finally, remember that positive reinforcement of good behaviour is the best educational measure of all.

Chapter 6
Step 3: Associative Training

STEP 3:
ASSOCIATIVE TRAINING

Associative training is all about making meaningful requests, and not empty demands, to your dog. As we've seen already, dogs have very good long-term memories – too good! In order for your dog to understand what your signals mean, you must present your signals clearly and be consistent in your use of them.

When you ask your dog to do something – for instance, sit or stay – he will respond by performing the task, performing it in a less than satisfactory manner or even by completely ignoring you. It is then up to you to deliver a consequence: either a positive stimulus for positive behaviour or a negative stimulus for negative behaviour. It's as simple as that, and is quickly and easily understood by your dog.

But what value do these skills have in a world that is full of complications, temptations and distractions for a dog? We need yet another element in our training.

Distractions as reinforcing tools

Is it enough to ask your dog to sit and he sits? Actually, no! You're not done yet. You need to reinforce your requests by adding yet another element: distractions. By introducing a variety of distractions, of different strengths, you bring your dog closer to making the only right choice when it comes to a real-life challenge. That is why it's much better to train outside, as I do with my clients, than in a church or community hall. I bring dogs with me to meet strangers and new dogs, and to encounter new situations. By allowing your dog to confront such distractions and then tackling his lack of focus on you when these present themselves, you'll be able to train him to respond more strongly and consistently to your requests.

Dogs need to be trained using all manner of distractions. Whether your dog is a city or country dog, he will need to be at ease with horses and dozens of other distractions.

For instance, most dogs love balls and want to chase them (although you can use any type of distraction that you want, such as a piece of meat or cheese, or a favourite toy). Ask your dog to sit and throw a tennis ball near him at the same time. Will he continue to sit? Probably not. Most likely, he'll want to go after the ball. So how do you get him to not go after the ball but continue to sit? By rewarding him when he doesn't go after the ball, of course, as well as by informing him that going after the ball is wrong when you've asked him to do something else.

Impossible, you say? Not at all. Every day when I walk my doggie pals, I ask them all to sit while I toss a ball. They've learned not to move a muscle until I release them. Then glorious mayhem breaks out!

You must always start training from the simplest level, so there is an exercise, in two parts, that I'd like you to do.

Dealing with distractions

Distractions training exercise 1. Ask your dog to sit as you stand facing him. Repeat the command and drop a titbit – as if by accident – somewhere out of his reach. Wait a couple seconds to

see if he is going to comply with your wishes or s.
temptation, then deliver the appropriate stimulus: positive
complies and stays in the 'sit' position; negative if he goes for the b.
If he does the second, you'll have to be quick to stop him getting at
it. Covering it with your hand or holding him back by stepping on
his lead is usually enough to convince him to trust and listen to you
the next time. Repeat this exercise as often as is needed for you and
your dog to succeed eight or nine times out of ten.

Well done! Your dog has started working on his own. You no longer
have to repeat your command, hold him back or eyeball him as you
worry about him staying put. You just ask him and he resists temptation
and, instead, pleases you. Isn't it a wonderful feeling? This is one of
the highlights of being a successful trainer.

Before we go on to the second stage of the exercise, let's look at a
case study that illustrates this first part.

SEBA

Seba is a pretty German shepherd and was about four and a half
months old when we started reinforcement training. His owners,
Bunshri and Kashi, had never had a dog before but a family member

always had German shepherds, so they decided to get one too. They made a good choice. Seba was a very bright and lovable pup. They started Hand Feeding him at about three months. By his fifth one-to-one training session, the penny had dropped and he was consistently responding to the persistent and consistent signals of his owners.

When introducing reinforcement training, I often use a long line. The dog is attached to one end and I'm at the other. When working with Seba, I had Bunshri or Kashi call him to them. After a while, when Seba was making an effort to come to me, I dropped a squeaky toy or a piece of food – both are very tempting for a young dog. He was just a puppy – and he hadn't mastered the skill of ignoring his owners yet! – so he only needed a bit of insistence at the start. Sometimes only a few gentle checks on the lead were all that was required for him to get the message. (Adult dogs don't need much more, by the way. The check is meant to be a nuisance to the dog and to alert him that something's not right with his behaviour.) We tried not to let Seba get to the toy or treat we had used as a distraction, otherwise he would have felt that he'd won a reward for doing something right. When he understood that he should go to his owners, he was rewarded generously with another treat, a bit of playtime with a toy, a hearty pat on the back and then one more treat.

After Seba had successfully come to me and ignored the distraction object consistently, we then made it into an even more enjoyable game. Still using the long line, we threw a ball and let him get it. He complied happily, like a good pup. We did this a few times before we told him, halfway through his chase of the ball, 'Stay!' If he continued towards the ball, all we had to do was press a boot down on his lead to stop him. We threw the ball again, and again asked him to stay when he was on his way towards it. Once more we stepped on his lead if he continued to move and head towards the ball. If he stayed still, Bunshri or Kashi went to him and rewarded him.

This is precisely the kind of exercise that builds up the strength of your dog's response to the commands you might use in an emergency in particular. By this I mean any situation where he is off the lead and you need to give him specific instructions for his safety.

By Seba's fifth lesson he was doing all this like a pro, thanks to his owners' diligence. It was now up to us to continue to give him more interesting things to do to expand his mind and his problem-solving powers.

Now let's return to that exercise:

Distractions training exercise 2. Training can become predictable for your dog and can reduce his motivation. To be predictable in training is to be a failure. The following exercise will leave you just as surprised as your dog by how impulsive you can be.

Start by having your dog adopt a sit or stand position by your side. Toss a biscuit a foot or so away from him and simultaneously ask him to change position. You'll probably not succeed the first time. He will, predictably, go after the treat.

Instead of correcting him, try using a positive stimulus in the form of a reward, or rather a bribe, to win him over. Take a very attractive piece of food to him – a piece of sausage, for instance – and when he is making a decision about whether or not he should go after that treat you threw on the ground, place the sausage close to his nose and bribe him into position, just as we did in the very beginning of our training. As always, use lots of rewards and practise lots of repetitions, and see what happens. You'll succeed in taking a bite out of a bad habit simply by using a reward. Take note of what and how it happened and how your dog reacted.

During my practice sessions I always bring one or another distraction tool to use while working my trainees. You can be as creative as you wish. Kick a football around while your dog is doing his stays. Use frisbees and whistles. Spread out cheese slices or crisps. Open your fridge and decide what the distraction *du jour* will be and go out and have a great time with your dog!

Some dogs that complete an exercise correctly will succeed the first time in a variation of the exercise. How do they know what is expected of them? It's called the rule of generalisation. They are able to rationalise that what they have done before is required once more. In practice, we need your dogs to have strong and reliable generalisation skills so that whatever unexpected event occurs, he'll think, 'Hum, it's probably just another set-up' or, 'That tempting object is just not worth the effort because listening to my master is more rewarding.' That's the whole idea – the holy grail – of this sort of training.

To illustrate, Matley, a boisterous German shepherd–Rottweiler rescue cross spotted two policemen on horseback on patrol through the fields. He took off after them, but about 50 yards into his chase he heard the command 'Come!' Guess what happened? He skidded, nearly falling over himself to turn around and rush back to the 'present' position. What a good boy! I don't think he'd ever seen horses before, but he generalised that 'come' meant just that, no matter what temptations lay ahead.

To build up your dog's generalisation skills, try some of these exercises at home. Make sure your pupil feels it's all right to resist temptations, because following your cues will bring him far better rewards and a better time overall.

• Recall through a corridor filled with treats (he shouldn't be ingesting them on his way back to you!) – first on the lead, then off

• Heelwork on a court filled with tennis balls

• 'Stays' with frisbees thrown over his head

• The 'down' position with biscuits on his paws

• Lead-following in a garden centre or pet shop

• Training at your local dog-training club with all their favourite routines.

If you want to perfectly reinforce your dog's understanding and obeying of a command, I advocate using ten distractions for each word you teach him. That's ten *different* distractions for each request. This requires a bit of creativity on your part, but once you get going, the possibilities are endless. Just remember always to keep your dog's safety, and that of others, in mind as paramount.

When training your dog in a park to achieve generalisation of a stay or other command, never use squirrels as the distraction. You're doomed to fail, as they are an irresistible temptation for most dogs. Squirrels need to be built up to over a lot of time and practice. By all means, go to the park and use other dogs, people and bikes (safely) as a distraction, but start off modestly and work your way up. Make sure the exercises you do with your dog are safe for you, him and everyone else around you.

Chapter 7
Step 4: Active Socialisation Under Supervision

All the good things that have come to me have come through my dog.
A dog owner overheard in New York's Central Park

Supervised socialisation encourages good behaviour for the future.

STEP 4:
ACTIVE SOCIALISATION UNDER SUPERVISION

Many trainers, including Dr Ian Dunbar, believe the critical period for socialising your dog ends at about three months of age. This means that at eight weeks of age – about the time when you get your new puppy from the breeder – he is nearly two-thirds of the way through his socialisation period. If the breeder hasn't been socialising your puppy with children, people and objects surrounding him, as well as with other dogs, you may encounter problems arising from the lack of socialisation. For this reason I recommend that you ask about the socialisation your pup has been getting *before* you take him home. And even though you may be reassured by the answer you get, you should start socialising your dog at the earliest opportunity.

A puppy's personality continues to mature, but at a slower rate, after this critical period has ended. By the age of five or six months, his behaviour is mostly formed, his preferences sorted, his survival rules established.

You must take an active role in your dog's socialisation. You're making a mistake if you think you can just throw him into a group of dogs and he'll learn everything he needs to in order to behave acceptably. It doesn't take long for a puppy to realise that if he's a little faster, a little cheekier, a little nosier than the other puppies in his training classes, he'll win more treats, toys and praise. Similarly, it doesn't take long for timid and shy pups to learn to seek protection and relish the comfort and safety from bullying by other dogs. This experience quickly gets reinforced very strongly in a puppy's mind because it is getting him what he wants. A strong pup learns to dominate by trial and error. This can begin as early as when he is suckling. He will nudge his weaker siblings out of the way, winning first dibs at mealtimes.

Resocialisation is even more fraught with difficulty. Many of my clients bring their dogs along to group training hoping to reintroduce them to the dog community. But without proper supervision and a re-education on the part of the client, what these aggressive or fearful dogs learn instead is that they are on their own with no one to stand up for them. If they lunge at another dog and their owners either let them or pull them back to safety, the dogs are learning that they themselves are controlling the situation – not the desired effect, I'm afraid. It's we owners who need to be in control at all times.

Pups Dexter and Benson having a safe play date.

As humans we often make the mistake of seeing this strong and competitive behaviour as something good. We will praise him, encourage him. 'Look at Benjamin. He gets the ball every time! Well done, Benny!' But this behaviour, left unchecked, can produce much more negative behaviour as the dog ages, including possessiveness, excessive competitiveness, growling, biting and barking.

Just like we humans, dogs need to learn how socialise with everyone for a peaceful existence for one and all.

I prefer to first introduce puppies into a structured, well-organised pack of adult dogs. They slip into place quite easily and don't go over the top, because of the control exerted by the older and better-behaved dogs as well as the leadership of their handlers and myself. Such an environment is also very useful in teaching your pup the basics of obedience training. Through copying the behaviour of his older comrades, a puppy can, for instance, learn recall, stays and retrieving.

So what do you do with a young pup and how do you begin to socialise him? I run puppy group classes where owners and their pups play games and the humans learn how to communicate their expectations. The classes are supervised and very structured. While the pups are playing these instructional games, they are also learning how to behave properly with one another. In this 'socialisation under supervision' process your dog will learn the right associations, how to communicate in an acceptable manner and to ask for guidance when he doesn't know what to do next.

When a large puppy, say a German shepherd, plays with a smaller puppy breed, like a dachshund, the dachshund will most likely get tired of the big pup's rough-and-tumble play and hide behind his owner for protection until he learns that a growl and nip work quite well to keep big oafs away from him – hence the origins of 'small dog syndrome' (the canine equivalent of the 'Napoleon complex'). You have to be knowledgeable enough to create an atmosphere where such things won't happen. You as an owner must step in and cut out that behaviour before it manifests itself in further aggression, perhaps against people.

There are many cases of small dogs sitting under dining tables and biting people's feet and legs when they move or get too close. Now you know where the behaviour started: in improperly supervised play sessions. Such dogs need to go through (or return to) the Hand Feeding programme to learn how interesting it is to exercise their brains while eating from the palm of their owner's hand. It may take a little while, but soon such dogs will be happy to interrupt their own activities to report to their handler when the opportunity is given.

Many dog owners I've encountered have become the night-walkers I mentioned earlier. Their dogs have become antisocial because, at some time in their early lives, their behaviour developed in its own way without the right guidance and stimuli. In these cases the unlucky owners have to cope with the negative consequences: their dogs have become aggressive or too risky to be around other dogs. The responsible owners have had to compromise and walk their dogs at night so that they can have peace and quiet on their walks and not have to worry about encountering other dogs or people (except for the other night-walkers!) and getting into situations that they are unhappy with or don't know how to manage. This is a management technique and at least the owners are doing what they can to keep their dogs out of trouble. If the only choice is between this and not taking these dogs out at all, I choose the night-walking plan. But it isn't the only option available to those who feel they can commit to solving their dogs' problems.

Happily, there is hope for older dogs to become resocialised properly. The same principles apply to older dogs as to puppies. Supervised group classes are extremely helpful because your dog can get an intensive 'socialisation workout'. I run a Saturday general group class at Sunnyhill Park and morning classes for rescue dogs at the RSPCA Southridge centre and anyone can come with their dogs, no matter how badly behaved they are. Because the groups are supervised and structured, the dogs quickly learn that not only is attacking other dogs very bad form, but it's much more enjoyable to play games with Mum and Dad, like recall, jumping relay races, musical chairs, egg-and-spoon and fetch. Hand Feeding and other games are substituted for aggression. With the steady patience of the owners, badly behaved dogs quickly turn their behaviour around and even look forward to classes and to the next play session with their owners and dog mates. In these classes I've rarely met a dog that finds it a thrill to nip at other dogs, so they are just as happy with this change of focus as the owner is. It is up to us as owners to make every day and every walk as enticing as possible.

'My dog doesn't like the postman.' 'My dog doesn't like children.' 'My dog doesn't like men with beards [or umbrellas or black hats].' I hear it all. But that doesn't mean your dog has to hate these things for ever. You can condition him to thoroughly enjoy, or at least happily tolerate, all of the above and any other pet peeve he has.

If you want to modify your dog's behaviour at a later stage, you have to understand how to build positive associations. For instance, in socialising your dog you want to teach him what to do with other dogs, people, children, cars and so on, rather than what *not* to do. When you and your dog are at a puppy party, how do you want him to behave? Reward anything that resembles good behaviour.

By building the associative understanding of events and objects, we try to condition what was previously irrelevant and meaningless to your dog to become relevant and meaningful. We can do this *directly* – your postman brings your dog goodies and so your dog likes him, so the reward is directly associated with the postman; or *indirectly* – the postman comes, you reward your dog for sitting and giving him your paw. The reward is directly a result of sitting and giving his paw, and positively, if indirectly, associated with the postman.

We can condition our dogs to believe that events or situations that are accompanied by something pleasant are things to look forward to. By using aversion techniques we can develop in a dog dislike or avoidance of a situation. Admittedly, it's easier said than done, for, as we said earlier, many dogs haven't learned to appreciate the attention from their handlers and therefore don't accept any form of reward and don't look forward to receiving one. Fortunately, as you now know, all such dogs can be persuaded to develop the right training spirit.

In my opinion, the best way to build positive associations for your dog is to teach him to be better reward-motivated (any form of reward will work but food is the easiest to use and the most reliable). If he is reward-motivated, you have a way in which to teach him the difference between good behaviour and bad. This is yet another arena where learning and training by Hand Feeding are so important.

If your dog doesn't take rewards or doesn't value them enough, is choosy, uninterested, not well bonded with you or doesn't respect you, forget it. You'll be wasting your time and money on something that otherwise should take you a few days or at most a couple of weeks to accomplish. Start by teaching yourself how to motivate your dog – this is the key to success. Condition your dog to want to learn, to want to have that reward and to appreciate it deeply, and you'll be most of the way towards modifying his unwanted behaviour. You'll never experience severe problems with a compliant and agreeable dog – a dog that looks right up into your eyes even before you ask him anything. Such a dog is thrilled to do whatever you ask because you've given him cause to – once he's been conditioned to, of course.

And once you've succeeded in socialising or resocialising your dog, remember that this condition requires maintenance. Just as you can't expect correct reactions from your dog unless you keep refreshing his training, so you can't expect him to continue to be well socialised, even if his critical period was correctly handled, without some upkeep. And let's face it, once you've discovered the pleasure of being out with other well-behaved dogs and their owners, you'll want to keep it up anyway.

MEGAN

One of my clients, Margaret, has a Jack Russell named Megan, who was a scrappy teenager when I met her. Apparently, people gave the two of them a wide berth as Megan was so unsociable. Megan is now seven and you'd never know she had been such a terrible terrier. Margaret brings her to most of our Sunnyhill Park group classes and she has performed in several of our display days, where my amateur dog handlers demonstrate the rewards of responsible dog ownership. But Megan's story is best told by Margaret herself. The following letter, abridged, appeared in our Winter 2000 newsletter.

I'm writing this for anyone who thinks — as I did until now — that it's only puppies and their young owners who are susceptible to training. My Jack Russell is four and a half, and I — well, let's just say I've had my free travel pass for more than ten years.

I adopted Megan when she was two. She came to me after an overnight journey from Wales in a van that had been on a rescue mission to the puppy farms. She'd then spent two nights at a sanctuary called, ominously, Last Chance. Thin, dirty, she was so pleased (it seemed) to make her home in my flat that I spoiled her from the start.

For various good reasons I had to keep her on the lead and away from other dogs for a good part of our first year together and by the end of the second she had developed some seriously antisocial behaviour. Someone told me that I had ruined her life by the way I had treated her and that it was far too late to remedy this.

Soon after I had to take her to the vet for her annual booster and as we walked into the waiting room full of silent, perfectly behaved animals the noise that came from Megan was deafening. We were quickly banished to a storeroom where we sat alone, in disgrace.

When the vet came to us (he wasn't going to risk another outburst) he said no one [should have to] put up with any more of this and gave me a scrap of paper with four capital letters and a telephone number on it. Greatly apprehensive, I called the number and made an appointment to meet Dima...

To my surprise and intense relief, Dima brushed aside my excuses, feelings of guilt and so on, and started work. I can't remember now exactly what we learnt that first day; I just remember feeling reassured. Five days later, we went to our first Group Session at Sunnyhill Park...

The exercises were in full swing. As we went through the gate, Megan's shrieks reached a new pitch of hysteria. I paused, expecting instant expulsion. But Dima picked her up, carried her around unconcerned while continuing to conduct the class, and by the end, on a very long lead and in a soft muzzle, Megan was beginning, almost, to be quiet. The other human members of the class were kind and forgiving and put me at ease.

In retrospect, it seems that Megan's subsequent transformation happened very quickly, but I suppose it took another three to four weeks and is still ongoing. What did happen was that I began to see signs of change and I stopped worrying. That communicated itself to Megan, who relaxed... I stopped growing tense the minute another dog came near, and Megan's hackles stopped rising, as her fears subsided.

I realise now that in our individual training sessions and the fortnightly Group Sessions Dima was not just asking us to do mechanical exercises. He was showing Megan and me how to use our brains, and making me see that Megan's much smaller brain functions quite differently from mine. Irrational as it might sound, I had got so used to chatting silently to her in my mind on our solitary walks in the park that when I did speak to her I used several words (yes, I have to admit, sentences) to explain why I didn't want her to do such and such a thing (like 'Megan, darling, try not to pull while this nice man is watching').

We've been training with Dima, off and on, for about four months now. Megan is much happier, and her excitement becomes ecstasy every other Saturday before we set out for Sunnyhill Park (how does she know what day it is?). Other dog-walkers no longer change course when they see us coming; there are smiles of welcome and praise for Megan – which she likes, though she prefers titbits. It's never too late to learn...

Chapter 8
Step 5: Companionship

If you don't own a dog, at least one, there is not necessarily anything wrong with you, but there may be something wrong with your life.
Roger Caras, *A Celebration of Dogs*

Dima with his friend, Benson.

STEP 5:
COMPANIONSHIP

Congratulations! Now that you have all the practical tools to train your dog, you can enjoy his companionship for the rest of his life. Through training – or, to put it another way, playing and spending time with and teaching your dog – you develop a clear way of communicating with him, and this can only produce a stronger and more satisfying relationship between you.

When I sent out a questionnaire to my clients asking for their assistance in the preparation of this book, Wendy, the owner of a Staffordshire bull terrier named Rufus, summed up the training process and its rewards perfectly. She said that kindness makes it pleasurable for both the dog and trainer; and that, through training, Rufus has come to enjoy the companionship of his human family and they him.

For some, this companionship extends to competing with their dogs. Indy is a wonderful example of how a dog becomes the positive centre and focus for his family.

INDY

Indy is a Great Dane who was selected with great care by Andrea and Gary and their daughters Natalie and Sasha. He is a handsome chap with a fine pedigree – his grandmother was Natasha, a blue Dane who had a role in *Elizabeth* with actress Cate Blanchett. It was when a relative's Great Dane came to stay that Natalie decided that the breed was the one and only for her. She vowed to save up enough to buy a puppy and with her parents' help it wasn't long before they had acquired Indy.

Indy settled into their home quite quickly, but when he started to really grow they began to have problems – mostly because other people saw him not as a puppy but as a full-grown dog and were nervous around him.

And this is when I first became acquainted with Indy and his family, who all wanted to be involved in his training. He had become the centre of their attention. A better family I could not have imagined. I knew from their devotion that Indy had found himself an excellent home where he could grow and prosper – and I don't mean just in size.

As they had thoughts of showing Indy one day, I thought it best to get him started on clicker training to speed up his learning and sharpen his skills. Even Sasha, at only ten years of age, joined in happily and got clicking with the rest of them.

Very quickly their diligence and enthusiasm paid off. At 22 months Indy was on the cover of the June 2003 issue of *Dogs Today*. The magazine credited his family:

Indy has the sort of presence you rarely encounter. As you can see, he is breathtakingly beautiful and in peak condition.

What you can't see is he was completely in tune with his owner and willing to do whatever she asked with tremendous style.

He was so very calm, too – I would say serene.

Indy's family is wonderfully dedicated to him and his education. They have been doing one-to-ones with me for a few months, and are regulars at our group classes. They attend other obedience classes as well, and practise at ring-craft club. Recently they have done a bit of showing with Indy. They entered him into the Harrow Show, where he won a first in the Non-Sporting Open class, and then to their great delight, he won Best in Show. Natalie wrote to me, brimming with pride, to say that his prize was presented by the Mayor of Harrow and that he got a beautiful rosette and a big trophy to match:

Indy behaved so well and ran around the ring so beautifully. I was really proud of him and Dad. Then we walked around and all of your training came into play, as so many people came up to him to stroke him we could barely move more than an inch at a time. He was excellent with the many young children and toddlers who came up to stroke him, too!
– Nat and a very tired Indy.

Dog display for the Heath and Hampstead Society.

Whether or not you compete with your dog, the point is to enjoy him in any way you can. Maybe you like to go camping together, go running, play pitcher, compete in agility, do heelwork to music or just take long walks. Whatever you like to do, do it together and make sure your dog is always safe.

But even now, with all your new-found knowledge, and the many hours of practice and energy you've put into your training to make your dog the stellar and wonderful creature he is today, your job isn't done. It never will be. You'll always have to ensure that you look after him in the best possible way. You'll always have to provide him with all the TLC he deserves, update your knowledge of maturation, old age and his health requirements, as well as keep up his activity level and mental stimulation.

Your dog has become dependent on you and therefore you'll have to (and I assume *want* to) include him in all your future plans, commitments, activities and probably even holidays. You'll have to calculate and learn how to handle his personal bills (insurance, vet fees, grooming, boarding and travelling costs) as they won't go away, and many of the costs will increase as he ages.

But now it's time to sit back and enjoy the gift of having a well-balanced, smart, socially and family-oriented dog. Think of all the things you can do together: outings, parties, competitions, group walks and even doggie holidays.

Every year the Good Boy Dog School conducts a dogs' training camp in Norfolk at a wildlife preserve campsite where, 24/7, we can do supervised, off-lead practice sessions. I ran a similar camp back home in the Ukraine but started my first one here in 2001. Over the years we've perfected our regimes and tactics to bring together shy and lonely pooches with pushy and aggressive hounds, as well as people all of kinds – confident or not – to live in harmony. We give our dogs endless opportunities of choice and freedom, with a million interactions each day. We train in a natural, most comprehensive, encouraging and stimulating way, covering all aspects of conditioning, reconditioning, flooding, desensitisation and reinforcement – all in approximately a week-long schedule.

At the training camp we practise our training and address problems in a variety of settings – from river walks to clay pigeon shoots (for loud-noise desensitisation), water and jet skiing (and you can try it too), horseback riding (not with the dogs, but they watch and learn how to behave) to partying with our dogs at medieval banquets and at singalongs round the campfire. We also practise heelwork to music and do agility training.

But the real point of the whole event is to enjoy our dogs in as many creative ways as we can. By opening up and presenting possibilities, we can build deeper and stronger bonds with our best friends, our dogs. (For information on camp dates, as well as all our training classes and newsletters, see our website, www.goodboydogschool.com.)

Rescue dog Fred got great training right away
from his owners Karen and Ian.

PART 3
BEST BEHAVIOUR

Mud-splattered border collie, Sebastian.

Chapter 9
Top Behavioural
Problems Explained

*I wonder what goes through his mind when
he sees us peeing in his water bowl.*
Penny Ward Moser

Dogs are influenced by their owner's lifestyle, their environment and what is commonly called self-education, which means they attain knowledge and use it always to their advantage – not always to your liking. It is of no relevance whether it was you who educated your dog or someone else before you.

So who is to blame for your dog's bad behaviour? Dogs are born with this *modus operandi*: see it, try it, and if you like it, remember it and do it again. Similarly, if they try it and don't like it, they will go off and try something else. When you're able to interrupt this pattern of behaviour, you're on your way to teaching your dog what is correct behaviour and what is not. So it makes sense to start to teach him where it is OK to sleep the moment he walks through your door rather than having to tell him to get off the bed, sofa or silk cushions later on. Teach him that coming back to you is rewarding for him, rather than having to tell him off every time he runs off oblivious to your calls. Teach him that peeing outside is even better than Christmas, instead of having to teach him where not to do his business. Teach him that walking on a slack lead makes for an enjoyable walk, instead of having to teach him not to pull.

Leo, an eleven-year-old ex-problem rescue dog.

You may be lucky and never have to know how to train your dog out of bad habits. But don't be disappointed if you do because *it's never too late to teach your dog right from wrong.* And, as the saying *should* go, it's never too late to teach an old dog a new trick.

I work a lot with difficult dogs. I run a training school with the RSPCA for their re-homed canine clients and I also work with many dogs from Battersea Dogs' Home and other rescue centres in Britain. Many of my individual clients are people who have acquired their dogs from rescue centres and shelters, giving them a second (or third, fourth, fifth or even sixth) chance. In my experience, no matter how severe a dog's behavioural problem, 99% of the time it's man-made. Yes, it's actually we who are the guilty party because we – and those who have lived with our dog before us in the case of re-homed pets – are instrumental in forming his inner world. And we do this every day, consciously or not.

All dogs think whatever they do is fine, otherwise they wouldn't act the way they do. Their behaviour must first suit them, as no dog will do anything that isn't to their advantage. They don't distinguish right from wrong until they are taught properly to come when called, stay at a distance, and not to jump on the sofa, chew up your slippers, chase the postman and wee on the carpet.

Many people don't know how to train a dog or even appreciate that training, formal or informal, is crucial. Like children, dogs don't come with a set of instructions. I may provoke wrath for equating babies with dogs, but most people attend pre-natal classes when they're going to have a baby, so why don't most people who have a dog take classes on caring for him and being a responsible owner?

Canines have an extraordinary ability to adapt to the lifestyles and circumstances they are put in. It's up to us to tap in to this finely tuned, built-in equipment when raising our dogs. Dogs have many more complexities than, say, flowers, although if you'll permit me to use the analogy, training dogs is a lot like raising plants: if you can get them from a very young age, you have the opportunity to nurture them so that they grow in the right way from the start.

It is up to dog owners to be responsible, *at all times*, for the safety both of our dogs and those who live around us. Acting in any other way will only turn public opinion against dog ownership and the freedoms we enjoy with our dogs. Dog ownership is a privilege and one that must not be taken for granted, far less abused. The more reckless individuals are with their dogs, the more likely dog owners, as a group, will be blamed and our liberties suspended or even taken away. By training your dog properly, you'll be doing your bit to make dogs and their owners welcome in our communities and parks.

Why You're Responsible for Your Dog's Behaviour

Dogs are never perfect, and at the Good Boy Dog School we believe that blaming them for their poor behaviour is wrong. They simply need proper instruction, and dog owners must provide them with all the training they need. I repeat: it isn't the dog that is at fault; it's us. I can hear the indignation now… 'Are you saying I'm responsible for my dog chasing after rabbits, chewing up my slippers and attacking the postman?' Quite truthfully, yes. Why? Because often we've failed to introduce proper instruction at the proper time and have left our dogs uninformed about what is the right way to cope with life's events.

This is even more evident with rescue dogs. Their owners understandably want to coddle them, especially if they were abused in their last home, and tend to ignore and *allow* their bad behaviour. Many of us accommodate and even reinforce our dogs' problems and faults – stealing, whining, barking in the house and so on – often without realising it. More often than not, dogs have the uncanny ability to outmanoeuvre us and win. We're willing hostages! Call it laziness or soft-heartedness, it doesn't matter. Dogs win and they remember and learn from it. They get used to winning – regardless of whether it matches our expectations – and to not being obliged to behave in any particular way but that dictated by them. And the more often they win, the more convinced they become that what they are doing is right.

We live by the same rules, do we not? If something works, we stick with it. If it doesn't work, we abandon it. But always there are the rules of society that dictate our actions. It is our rules that must dictate our dogs' actions – both for their safety and the happiness of our coexistence.

Dominance

The word 'dominance' is used to explain many unwanted behaviours, especially aggression, but it is widely overused and very unhelpful. As professional trainer Samantha Scott says:

• 'Dominance' doesn't mean you have to *bring your dog to heel* by being tougher than he is.

• The word doesn't help in working out the cure.

• Either a dog is dominant or he is not – if he is the former he will display dominant traits in all aspects of life, not just in one or two, which is most often the case.

Dominance is all about survival, and a true alpha dog, of which I've seen very few, doesn't need to display his status by 'acting out'. Such dogs are socially superior, so they don't need to be pushy or aggressive towards other dogs. It's a big job being on top and most dogs don't want the responsibility. It's hard work! Many dogs end up taking up the post simply because the humans in their lives aren't picking up the ball, so to speak. Scott compares us to dogs in that we're both social predators. And, like dogs, most of us don't want to be chief executives or have great responsibilities. But we all want the enticing pay packages! And so do dogs. The instinct to compete and earn more benefits than those in the lower ranks is present in any animal.

The way to achieve these benefits isn't always through dominance; respect and appreciation may also play a part. How do our dogs know how to earn these extra benefits? Instinct, of course, but trial and error is also vital in their decision making.

So what is all this behaviour that we think of as dominant, like aggression towards other dogs, possessiveness, protectiveness? Most often it isn't, in fact, dominance, but pushiness, manipulation, arrogance and even the result of stress. It is learned. And it is especially evident when a dog is getting everything he wants. Therefore, if this 'power play' is learned, we can educate the dog to modify his behaviour. We can divert his conduct to enable him to think and act in a positive, pleasing manner. And if we're good teachers we will act proactively instead of waiting for bad behaviour to rear its ugly head.

Gentle leaders versus dictators

Life is like dog sledding. If you are not the lead dog,
the scenery is always the same.
Anonymous

Take charge and be your dog's leader.

So what can we do about dominance in our dogs? Do we have to be dominant to get them to do what we want them to do? Some owners may feel satisfied with this, but I believe it is the least attractive solution. Dominance is counterproductive in our relationships with dogs, who are our friends and members of our family. It's wrong in a relationship that is really about communication and caring. We don't want to be heavy-handed about it.

As Pam Whyte tells us in *Living with an Alien:*

Commands and punishment aren't what leading a pack is all about. Where there is defective leadership, there is a lot of rebellion and disobedience, so it is a sign of FAILURE when we shout and get angry and 'have to' do a lot of disciplining.

And our dog knows it. If he obeys because he is scared, we aren't a leader, but a dictator. And dictatorship is failed leadership.

Consider for a moment why at times you'll see a young child easily leading a dog through a busy park while a burly body-builder type needs a choke chain on his dog but still fails to win the dominance game. At the Good Boy Dog School we employ the power of the mind to prove that leadership doesn't require physical strength.

We want to be gentle leaders, not dictators, but I realise this can be very difficult for the many people who are happier not taking on the job. Most of us aren't born leaders. But if you want your dog to be well behaved and happy, you'll have to step up to the doggie bowl!

Dogs demonstrate their status to other dogs in many ways. They stare, snarl, growl, put up their hackles, rise up on their toes, stiffen and move about in a cocky way, chase and nip, protect or deliberately pick on another dog. Responding slowly and ignoring such behaviour in other dogs are common ways of saying who is in charge. Humping or mounting another dog is another effective way of demonstrating superiority. Fighting, strangely enough, is such a rare occurrence that it is hard to consider it a way of establishing dominance. Getting hurt will affect a dog's ability to hunt and survive, as wounds can become infectious, and therefore these should be avoided at any price. Winning could cause prolonged suffering or even death. This is why dogs are such natural artists at the status game. They are such successful performers that we humans buy into their tricks. We label them problem dogs and grant them the privilege of getting what they want, providing them with routines that comfort them and that they demand, and even get out of their way.

What's the alternative? Meeting the challenge head on? Eyeballing your pooch? Growling at him over his feeding bowl? Outrunning him in pursuit of his tennis ball? Good luck to you if you think you can employ the techniques of the canine repertoire!

We aren't dogs, so it is impossible for us to use all the same social tools that they use to establish leadership. We just can't be convincing enough to fool them. Even if we knew what all these signals were we'd be hard-pressed to put them all to use practically and with the same skill. Nor would we want to put many of them into practice (bum sniffing, especially!). But, just as we're capable of using body language to demonstrate superiority over people, so we can use human tools to help us gain a leadership role in our relationship with our dog. Such tools, a few of which are listed below, can be used as supporting elements in your regular dog training. You know your dog best. If you know you have a very manipulative animal, you may have to be more persistent in flexing your leadership muscles. But it's up to you to decide how much muscle you need to put into your relationship and when. At the same time it's important that you assess whether or not you're successful in this role, and that you adapt to improve your standing if necessary.

Power play

Is your dog dominating you? Look for telltale signs like him hogging the couch while you get the floor!

Before I list the standard steps for building up your leadership status, I would like to tell you how I see all these established rules myself. I love dogs jumping up on me, although not on other people. All my family pets, including my setters and some of my dog lodgers, sleep in my bed and rest on the sofa. They climb on to my lap if they can. Some, like my beagle friend Aristotle, sit at a designated spot at the table. A few even eat at the table. I pick them up if I feel like it and play most of the stupid games they want to play with me.

When you've recovered from the shock of my revelations, I can tell you my excuse for my behaviour – the reason why I can do all this stuff with my dog pals: I make my own rules and have my own boundaries, just as you should. Some of the standard rules I like and so I use them. Others I don't like, so I don't use them.

I don't have any problems with dominance, as I implement my rules from day one of meeting a new dog. He quickly learns what I feel is good behaviour and what is bad. Some people learn how to do this quite easily, and perhaps it is simply instinctual. Others need more help and direction. If you fall into the latter group and need to know what to do, looking at the way the experts handle the status issue, as expressed in power play, will be very useful. Only do what you're comfortable with and what you feel you can use on a daily basis.

Ari all dressed up.

There are some key rules of human-dog engagement, and understanding these will allow you to assess where you fall on the leadership scale. Look at the following and make a note of areas where you may need to assert your power.

• Where does your dog sit in relation to you? You should sit in a higher position than him. If, for instance, he has your chair and you're sitting on the floor, you know you're in trouble!

• Who walks through doors first, you or him? If he's bursting ahead, he thinks he's leading the way instead of you. Encourage him to follow you.

• Do you eat before your dog does? Beware of the message you're sending him if you aren't. In the wild, the top dog gets the first crack at food. If you want to act like the alpha dog, you should too.

• Does your dog barrel through the doorway to greet visitors? You should be greeting them before he does. Reward him for staying quietly nearby until you give him permission to say hello.

• Can you sit in your dog's bed or sleeping area? Top dogs can sit and sleep wherever they want. Make sure that you can and that your dog asks for permission to sleep on your bed with you.

• Will your dog allow you to take his feeding bowl, even while he's still eating from it? If you're your dog's leader, you should be able to do this without a problem.

• Do you decide when it's playtime or does your dog only play with you when he feels like it? Keeping toys tucked away until you decide when he should have them and when you can play together will help you establish your leadership role (and will also make the toys more desirable to your dog).

• Are you being pulled down the street by your dog, or does he walk placidly and contentedly by your side, looking up to you for guidance? If it's the former, you need to change the rules. If you want to be your dog's leader, you have to guide him in every aspect of life, and this includes *all* your walks.

• Does your dog comply with all your wishes? Does he allow you to groom, bathe and handle him without any fuss? Dogs who resist such personal attention are resisting your leadership. You have to establish yourself as his guide, to get him to trust you in all circumstances.

Hand Feeding really pays off when you need to groom, inspect and touch your dog.

Shifting the balance of power

Some of the power games that are regularly advocated in traditional dog training are useful for tipping the scales in your favour. Review the following list and decide what will work for you:

• From day one, you must choose when you pet and cuddle your dog, not the other way around. A dog that is used to being engaged in your routine is your true follower.

• Don't get out of the way of your dog. Encourage him to move aside if he's barricading your way.

• Don't allow your dog to sit or stand on you. It's up to you to invite your dog to sit with you, not for him to say when and where.

• Don't get into a staring match with your dog when it's obvious he's trying to manipulate you (and not just staring up at you lovingly with devotion).

• Pet your dog with confident and decisive strokes. A light touch can project weakness and neediness on your part. Instil confidence that you're strong and in control.

• Practise opening your dog's mouth and examining his ears, paws and body. He should let you accomplish this without argument. All of him belongs to you and he should comply and believe it.

• At all times act with confidence and decisiveness. Your dog needs to feel he can look to you for help and guidance.

Above all, the name of the game is to *win*! At a recent lecture I gave called 'Who Trains Whom?', on behaviour modification for badly behaved dogs and their owners, I videotaped the attendees with their dogs as they arrived. Of note was one owner who was accompanied by a Patterdale terrier. As the owner was registering, his dog was pulling on his lead in every direction, like a maniac. The owner blissfully ignored this behaviour. Later in the evening I played back the film to talk about it with the class. Why was the dog acting this way? More to the point, why was the owner acting this way? Does he like having his dog pull him all over the place? No, of course not. He'd just become used to the dog pulling, didn't know how to resolve the problem and so let him have his way. He was letting his dog win and call the shots. Subsequently the dog really didn't do much that the owner asked of him. From bad recall to chasing, barking and attacking – he had all the baggage.

On a walk recently I came across a lovely spaniel puppy of about seven months who, after seeing the dogs with me (and who had done nothing threatening), immediately took fright. What did the owner do? He ran to his dog, hugged him and eventually picked him up and carried him away.

Now, I don't know why this dog had become frightened of other dogs – or rather why no one had taken steps to explain the situation to the dog in a logical way – but the fact that he was frightened was confirmed by the owner as we chatted briefly about his dog's behaviour. It was apparently 'a new development', but the owner couldn't place when it started. Being wary of the unknown is one of the most natural reactions for a dog and there was probably just one small incident, if any, that lay behind this dog's fear, and yet the owner took enormous pity on him.

What had the dog learned from this? That if he acts afraid of other dogs, he'll get his master's attention and sympathy and gain security. His owner has been taught by his dog to accommodate his behaviour.

What should the owner of such a dog have done instead? A good idea would be to take the pup to small group classes of well-behaved dogs to help him become friendlier. From the very beginning the owner needs to convey confidence to assure and gain the trust of his dog. He should use an upbeat reassuring voice to welcome other passing dogs, maybe give them a few steady pats on the head, while ignoring his dog's unwanted behaviour. He needs to demonstrate that he isn't afraid and act confidently and decisively for, in the end, he is the boss and is responsible for his dog's security and for educating and informing him of what to expect. At the same time, he needs to take away the positive reinforcement – cuddles and hugs – that the dog is getting in response to his timidity. Take away that and there will be little reason for the dog to want to act this way any more. When the dog decides to stop doing so, that's the time his owner should reward him. Hand Feeding such a dog, while using other dogs as a distraction, is also a very useful exercise here, as it instructs the dog on what to do and what not to do.

Another dog I know likes to ride in the front seat of the car, even if it means the human passengers must take the back. Otherwise, what happens? He incessantly barks and whines – essentially throwing a tantrum like a child who hasn't got his way. We know that when a child does this we should either give him a firm rebuke or ignore him. Certainly we shouldn't give in to him, because he'll win, and if he wins, this will only lead to further trouble. One thing is sure: we will lose control. Dogs aren't human, but their primary emotions work in a similar way. When they don't get their way, they can sulk, whine and generally make our lives miserable, tugging on our heartstrings and making us feel guilty. Worst of all, we often give in, letting them win. I have great sympathy here, as I do this all the time with my five-month-old son. I certainly need a baby trainer – someone to prepare me for all the challenges ahead.

I know it can be hard. Once they have discovered they can push their boundaries, dogs can be very creative in trying to get their way in many areas of our everyday lives. And they are so very cute and so very easy to spoil. The trick is to face them down. Never lose your temper; instead, be patient. Use your arsenal of tools to deliver a firm rebuke if need be, but overall, use positive reinforcements, like treats, to let him know when he's done something right. If he's begging at dinner, save a reward for him for returning to his bed or the living room, or for just settling down. Most importantly, follow your intentions consistently.

Winning also plays a major part in regular training. It isn't enough to ask your dog to sit, for instance, and he sits 85% of the time. You may not want a Cruft's obedience winner, but if you want your dog to listen to you all the time, you can't let him get away with that other 15% of the time when he ignores you and walks off to sniff under a bush. That 15% carries over into all other aspects of your relationship with your dog. He knows you aren't really in control, and this confuses him. He has to understand that when you ask him to do something it's not a multiple-choice question! 'Sit' should mean and always mean 'sit'.

So, to review, how do you win? *You win by being consistent, persistent and fair.* This is the language your dog will understand because your messages will be clear signals − not confused and incoherent requests. Add helpful accessories such as brainpower, knowledge, someone to consult with, enough time on your hands, the desire to get your training right and, obviously, the love of your dog, and you'll be winning in the training game in no time.

Hand Feeding (see p. 71) gives even the most inexperienced owner a guide of necessary steps to win by harnessing his dog's intelligence. This technique, above all others, provides you with the tools to play the game with all the aces in your hand. In the case of Hand Feeding, these cards truly lie in the palm of your hand: they are the rewards you give your dog for his correct behaviour, and they are the source of his motivation.

If you've followed diligently our guidelines on establishing that right attitude and attention in your dog, you should now be able to give advice to those in trouble. Reliability as the result of a strict and accurate training regime, practised with distractions and polished up with mild corrections, is the answer to all your questions.

Desensitisation

Your dog likes to chase joggers, attack motorcycles and bark at other dogs. Somewhere along the line he has decided that one or more of these, or countless others occurrences, is a thing that needs to be barked at. And as he has strengthened this association, it's now become learned. Jogger = Chomp at Heels; Postman = Snarl; Car = Chase.

What can you use of what you now know to help combat these issues? All that is required is a little creativity that tops up all that you know already. Now that your dog is food- or toy-motivated, why not use these to assist in the process of desensitising the stimulus you wish to erase?

Desensitisation aims to establish in your dog a more desirable response to irritants that may cause him to act fearfully – for instance, going to the vet, or hearing loud noises, like thunderstorms, cars, motorcycles, skateboards, fireworks, vacuuming, and so on. It is a process by which a dog is able to gradually overcome his fear. Desensitisation training involves initially exposing your dog to low levels of the irritant and, as he becomes more confident, increasing the intensity of the frightening stimulus to a point where his fearful response is eliminated. To accomplish this successfully, you must stop at each level before your dog reacts fearfully. Ignoring the stimulus, diverting the response and establishing new associations all serve the same purpose.

Let's say you're walking down the street and a thunder-busting Harley-Davidson rips by at full throttle, sending your dog into a frenzy. It would be nice if he didn't do that, you're thinking to yourself. Well, let's look at how a client of mine, Ann, solved this problem with her 'Heinz 57', Pepper.

Ann started by finding some parked motorcycles and taking Pepper over to them – not too close at first. She made him sit and do some other manoeuvres and started handing out treats, rewarding his good behaviour. The focus wasn't on the motorcycles, just good sits and stays and working together. Then Ann brought him closer to the bikes, gradually moving in until finally they were right next to them. Pepper's hesitation disappeared as he concentrated on how he was going to get more titbits.

Desensitisation is easy with a ball nut, like Bernard.

They had a few more sessions like this over a few days until Ann was satisfied that they could progress to moving motorcycles. The next time she went out she was actually hoping to see one! This being London, she didn't have to wait long. When the bike came into sight, Ann began putting Pepper through his manoeuvres, doling out the goodies as he did his stunts. They were so far away from the passing bike that it didn't provoke as much anxiety as before, giving Ann time to work on Pepper's road drill. She persisted, ignoring the small displays of bad behaviour that he exhibited over the next few sessions, and kept asking him to listen to her, patiently guiding him back to concentrating on her and the treats. Slowly he settled and went back to his training when the bike was in and out of sight but still quite a distance away.

Ann stuck to this routine for several weeks. And what do you know? Pepper is now cured of lunging at moving motorcycles. He seems to not notice them at all. These days he and Ann can walk happily down the road, incident-free – a great reward for their few weeks of work together.

The idea of desensitisation works perfectly on most bad habits that need to be simplified or brought to a manageable level. As Pepper's story shows, this can be accomplished by slowly establishing the desired response, gradually building it up to the necessary level to replace the formerly unmanageable response to the troublesome stimulus.

Diversion

The diversion technique is the most obvious illustration of associative learning. It uses indirect conditioning to provide the solution to your dog's problem.

One of our trainees, a strongly aggressive Weimaraner, would not tolerate large male dogs approaching him – unless he was kept busy doing something else. After being trained to follow most disciplinary exercises, we introduced the 'holding' command, which is similar to the one used to request retrieval. We managed to build up his holding skill to over ten minutes at a time, and when holding an object he would happily avoid any dogs and trot away, to his owner's great relief.

Ben, a 'Battersea special', a medium-sized black-and-tan dog, had never seen a horse in his life. His owner took training very seriously and after initial success started to enter him for obedience competitions. As the stay test requires, Ben would sit or lie and stay in practically any circumstance. So, when we had one of our socialisation classes booked up at a stable yard, we asked Ben to walk to heel as we passed the stabled horses or freeze his stays when horses were led by. He passed his horse tolerance test his first time out, and enjoyed the whole experience very much, thanks to the treats we used to reward his good behaviour.

Diverting behaviour is normally much easier than opposing the actual issue of disobeying or misbehaving, because you're able to rely on different and stronger response reactions from your dog. If he isn't great on his recall and is easily distracted, teach him to stay wherever he is. See if the problem is the 'come' command or if he is just ignoring you and your instructions. If it's the second, then forget about recall training. You need to go back for a Hand Feeding refresher (see p. 85) to firm up his attention so that he focuses on you.

Modelling

The technique known as 'modelling' is a very effective way to deal with many types of bad habits, to get your dog to acquire new patterns of behaviour, to strengthen or weaken responses already present in his behavioural repertoire, and to inhibit learned phobias and fears. It involves imitating, or recreating, the problematic situation in a training environment.

A Dachschund enjoying the summer flowers.

For instance, if your dog snuffs up everything off the ground like a canine hoover, you can teach him to stop doing so by the use of role-playing. In a controlled environment, place a treat on the ground and allow him to take it. Repeat. Now put a treat on the ground and tell him, 'No' or 'Leave it!' If he goes for the treat, deliver a correction. If he doesn't, praise him. It's as simple as that. Practise this with a variety of tempting treats, replicating as much as possible the things your dog likes to pick up off the ground. Get yourself a burger wrapper, a piece of chicken (without bones, of course) – anything you know he finds particularly tempting – and practise with these. Teach him that getting rewards from you for acting well is much nicer than getting nothing when he chooses to misbehave. Then you'll be ready to tackle his hoovering behaviour outdoors in a real-life situation. If he still tries to pick up litter, you can replicate your corrections and rewards as you did in the modelling scenario. If you practise diligently, the problem should disappear quickly.

There are many things you can do to promote good behaviour and to educate your dog. For instance, we go to a small zoo in a local park – where dogs are allowed if on the lead – to teach our trainees to accept other animals. Other exercises you can do on your own include teaching your dog to get used to fast-moving objects like squirrels and bikes by practising with stopping a ball game in mid-chase or coming away from frisbees. Use your creativity, and all the tools and various environments you have at your disposal.

Management solutions

Every aspect of your dog's unwanted behaviour has to be dealt with, because the compromises and sacrifices we have to make otherwise can turn dog ownership into a misery rather than the blessing it should be. It is pointless to show your dog at a dog event, enter him into competitions or engage in any similar activity if you can't even let him off the lead and be sure he'll return when you call him.

I'm absolutely certain that any healthy and happy dog can overcome all behavioural problems and become a well-adjusted and well-behaved one. But problems don't disappear if you ignore them. Instead, they develop, escalating until most of your dog-owning experiences are spoilt and having a dog becomes a hard and exhausting job.

Bad habits are self-regulating and self-reinforcing. The more you allow your dog to slack on his obedience routine, the more honed his skill at doing so will become. And then, without corrective training, there's no way out, as there is no reason for him to make a change or modify his behaviour. So what's the answer? It's simple. *Stop letting your dog get away with not responding properly to your commands.* If there is anything you can do, or not do, to invoke a stress-inducing reaction from your little rascal, do it!

There'll be no more 'How do I get him back?', as you shouldn't allow him to get away from you in the first place. Not a perfect solution or the one you were hoping for? I know, but if you have to compromise and choose between having your dog walk at all times on a long line and risking him getting run over by a car because he's off the lead, what are you going to choose?

If you have enough time and the right amount of commitment, determination and ambition, you can train away any bad behaviour. If your dog has poor recall, you won't be able to train him off the lead when he's off chasing rabbits in a field, but you can train him by first starting him on the Hand Feeding routine (see p. 71), then putting him on a long line and teaching him to return, gradually upgrading him to off-lead walking and recall from 100 yards away.

But there may be times when you'll have to compromise and learn how to deal with a not so perfectly behaved dog by *managing* his misbehaviour – for instance, crating him at night if he constantly wakes you up in the middle of the night. Therefore you have two choices when you wish to eliminate your dog's undesirable behaviour. You can train him to do what you want him to do instead. Or you can use a 'management solution' – a way to prevent the activity from occurring without directly addressing your dog's problem.

For instance, if he digs up your geraniums every time you leave him in the garden, you can:

• Not let him into the garden, or let him back in directly when he's finished his business.

• Use the special deterrent products that are currently on the market to spread around the area he likes to destroy.

• Only let him into the garden when you can be there to supervise him.

• Fence off all flower beds.

• Keep him occupied with something else – a toy, for instance.

With persistent use of any of these solutions you'll achieve the desired result. Furthermore, many of the habits don't come back after being eliminated from the dog's repertoire for some time. So this tactic can be used effectively as an indirect training tool.

For use in both management solutions and training there are literally hundreds of modern gadgets and remedies that have been developed to target troublesome dog behaviour. In fact, I don't think there is a problem for which some sort of a device hasn't been invented, either to deal with it or prevent it from occurring altogether. And as long as these tools are used correctly, I see no problem using them as supplements to your training. To take just three examples, a travel kennel is a useful tool for potty-training a puppy; a long line is handy for keeping your dog with you on a walk; and a muzzle is invaluable for resocialising a rescue dog or helping you to enjoy the company of your barker, destroyer or scavenger.

But do you need these tools? No. But why shouldn't you use them if they speed along the training process? Especially when you're addressing the behavioural problems of older dogs and rescue dogs, they can be very useful. But they are also beneficial for training young puppies too – for instance, to teach a pup that he mustn't chew your shoes. This habit idea will soon become disagreeable to him if they are either not available for him to chew or they are sprayed with a deterrent spray or clove oil.

I try to keep abreast of all the latest training aids and gadgets. The following is a short list of equipment I regularly use and/or recommend to my clients. I've also included here warnings about particular devices.

Halti®/Gentle Leader® head collar; body harness. The design of these items makes it almost impossible for a dog to pull when on the lead. It's best to have them fitted and adjusted by a professional, but after they've been on for just a couple of weeks they teach the dog that pulling on the lead is simply out of the question. Then their regular collars can be put back on.

The Halti and Gentle Leader are head collars that enable you to lead your dog by putting pressure on the head of the dog or his muzzle instead of on the base of his neck. Dogs' necks are very strong and the more they pull, the stronger the neck gets. This headgear prevents neck muscles building up in this way. When you're using a head collar, your dog's head, as he tries to pull, is automatically brought to the side, which is most inconvenient for him. So he learns not to pull when the device is on.

There are also harnesses that go around the dog's body (note that they aren't the kind used in dog sledding) and these often give owners more control. They aren't very comfortable for the dog, as they tighten in proportion to the strength of his pull.

Lunge line; long line; cord; training lead. These all come in various sizes, but I recommend using one of approximately 30 feet in length. They make sure that your dog stays with you instead of taking off on his own hunting or chasing, as it is simply not possible for him to do so. A happy and safe run-around with a 60-foot diameter is what we all want, isn't it? In time, the leads can be shortened, replaced and eventually, when the dog is desensitised to temptations, completely dispensed with. There are many fields of dog training and disciplines where these leads either come in handy or are invaluable.

Muzzles. Any type of muzzle – Baskerville, wire, plastic or soft – will allow you to act responsibly and feel safe. They also help to break bad patterns of eating rubbish and picking up all sorts of things, as well as behaving in an aggressive manner. Muzzles need to be properly fitted and adjusted to your dog. They're a very useful and beneficial tool, but it's a pity they have such bad associations among uninvolved parties and even many dog owners. (See Aggression and biting, p. 226.)

Taste and smell deterrents. There are many different kinds, using different ingredients, and, because these may be ingested by your dog, you should obtain a professional's approval before using one. They are proven to be effective ways to teach a dog about no-go or no-touch zones. Individually tested, they will work on some dogs and not others. We've found that clove oil or bitter apple-based products work better than others.

Anti-barking devices. These vary between countries and the choice you make is likely to depend on both your budget and your ethics. They range from tight muzzles that should only be used for short intervals to digitally operated complicated devices like ultrasonic collars and plugs-ins, to bark-activated spray collars.

But before you try any of these, I recommend using alternatives – stuffed and interactive toys and long-lasting chews, for instance – to help occupy a barker. These can replace his anxiousness and boredom by keeping him busy and focused on something else.

Toys. If you think your dog gets bored while you're away from home and therefore begins to bark or destroy things, you may want to rely on a 'thinking' toy to keep him busy. Putting treats in an Activity Ball, Buster Cube or other feeding cube, so that he has to push it around in order to get the treats out, is an excellent way to curtail boredom. You can even devise your own toy with a sock, some yarn and a few treats. Be creative to stimulate your mutt's brain.

Gretchen, a rescue dog, living a new, happy life in America.

For passionate chewers, there is a wide variety of attractive toys available. The Kong, for instance, is a very sturdy rubber toy that is claimed to be indestructible (at least in the black version) for even the most energetic, large-jawed chewers. You should also consider the various recipes you use for making the meals that you place in them, so that these last longer and are more fun for your dog.

Remote aversion devices. These include spray or ultrasound collars and will only work successfully in the hands of an experienced trainer. They are helpful for controlling the runaway, scavenger or attacker, or simply the over-friendly, jumpy and overexcited dog when he is at a distance from you.

These devices are expensive, however, and a long lead will do the job just as well. When a dog is faced with a reprimand or pulled away, he will, hopefully, abandon his mission and instead find something else to do that's more to your liking. If you use a positive approach, he'll concentrate on what he sees brings him pleasing results.

Travel kennel; puppy pen; stair gate; dog-guard. These all help to keep your dog contained at a desired time and will prevent him from chewing, destroying or swallowing unwanted objects.

They will also stop him running out of the house, stealing things or jumping up on people. Overall, they are invaluable for teaching young pups or newly re-homed dogs house and toilet manners. (I recommend you consult a professional about the use of confinement and appropriate times for use. Also, remember to exercise your dog regularly, as being restricted may not be good for him for any length of time. This equipment must always be used humanely.) Using any of these items that help promote boundaries may be your first step towards achieving the results you're seeking.

Make sure that you train your dog first on how to use them. A travel kennel, for instance, is supposed to be a place of comfort and safety. A dog that has been trained from a very early age to use one of these will often retreat there to get away from it all, have a little peace and quiet, or just to feel safe during, say, a thunderstorm. However, never use this device to discipline a dog, as all the benefits will be quickly erased, and on top of that, it's simply harsh to shut up an animal against his will.

To get your dog used to his kennel, take it slowly. Let him see you throw some fabulously delicious treats or his favourite toy inside. You may even wish to feed him there at mealtimes. Let him walk in on his own and eat the treats or fetch the toy. Whatever you do, don't slam the door behind him! Let him get used to it at his own pace. It may take several days, maybe longer. Just be patient and let him get used to it being around and having things he likes inside it. Eventually you'll be able to try shutting the door and walking away for a few minutes. When you return, always praise your dog and reward him for his new-found skill of being able to stay in his kennel and be comfortable there.

Tie-up post; clip-on ring or hook. These gadgets help your dog to learn how to stay in one spot (in the car boot, in bed, outside doing stays) without disobeying you. It doesn't require any training but gets the job done. Consider these items when you're uncertain whether your dog will stay put when you're bringing your shopping in, or while you're gardening or playing with children. After a few times he will learn to settle down in a particular spot when asked to do so.

Obstructions; repellents; electronic border guards. These devices, which include invisible fences or high-pitched blasts to mark out no-go areas, will teach your dog to stay only where he is permitted, even without your supervision. Their use is undoubtedly a quick solution, although proper training will accomplish the same job. You should also consider the alternatives first. My family used to leave a stool on the sofa where the dog attempted to sleep a few times in our absence, with the result that he didn't look for a place on the sofa any more. Make sure that whatever you use as a repellent or obstruction won't harm your dog.

There are many other solutions, but, before considering use of any deterrent device, bear in mind the important fact that a dog that is given enough to eat is less likely to steal food; a well-exercised pup is too tired to get into mischief; a confined dog can't be where is he isn't allowed; and a busy dog can not be in two places at once. Once you've established a good pattern, your dog is unlikely to try anything else. Why would he if he is happy with the way things are? And once you've broken any bad patterns and stuck to the new regime (for as little as two weeks in some cases), he is unlikely to go back to his old sins, simply because he hasn't been given the opportunity to indulge in them for some time.

You should also experiment with using experts. Giving your dog to a dog walker – even just once – may give you the management solution you're looking for, whether it be for walking him or keeping him quiet in the house. Using a dog minder in your absence is a good way to deal with destructive behaviour or noise nuisance. A groomer may be the answer for a dog that doesn't like to be washed and brushed; and regular, stress-free trips to the vet may help you teach your dog to accept strangers and take medicine.

These and many other people, both professionals and enthusiasts, have lots of experience and therefore will be able to use their knowledge to make their tasks easier when coping even with a dog that has had no training. By using specialised professionals, you'll be helping to socialise your dog, and you'll learn what dogs are all about.

Hiring a dog walker can be great fun for your dog.
Just look at all the friends he can make!

Ideally, though, you won't have to invest in most of the gadgetry out there if you have a puppy and have trained him properly from the beginning. The key is not to wait until you have problems and then have to sort them out, but to train the little fur ball correctly in the first place. Getting organised, and deciding which tools you'll need to teach your dog good behaviour and to correct unwanted behaviour as it materialises *before* your puppy arrives, is the best way to ensure you spend the least amount of energy and money trying to modify bad behaviour later on.[9] By providing your puppy with positive experiences right from the start – this toy is for chewing and this table leg is not – you're giving him clear guidance on what he is permitted to do. I'll say it again: you *don't* have to teach your dog what *not* to do, only *what* to do instead.

There are several critical stages of activities and responses in a puppy's development. You enter a race against time and you have to be one step ahead of your dog, prepared to create the right training environment. If you aren't, you'll be spending your time trying to reverse negative behaviour, which is both more time-consuming and not guaranteed to achieve complete change.

Separation disorders

However, if you haven't got it right with your puppy or you have an adult dog or rescue dog with problems, help is still at hand. I believe there are no lost causes; as long as a dog is healthy, you can, with a little time, patience and understanding, modify his unwanted behaviours.

Whether or not you've skipped to this section without reading all that came before, I'll be punishing you with repetition. As I've said and will continue to say, our Hand Feeding training (see p. 71), which so effectively builds communication between you and your dog and promotes you as your dog's gentle leader and educator, will be the root solution to most behavioural problems (aside from any that are medical in origin) you have with your dog.

According to Novartis Animal Health Group, an international health care company, there are over 6.5 million dogs in Britain and approximately 15% of them suffer from separation anxiety disorders. Likewise, in the USA, there are 52 million dogs, 14% of which exhibit some form of separation anxiety. That's seven million dogs! The result is costly damage to the home and garden, barking and howling for hours on end, and what is politely called 'inappropriate elimination'.

Of course, it *is* true that every day many dogs vandalise their owners' homes in their absence. Contrary to popular belief, however, only about 10% of these animals, at most, are actually clinically anxious. Most are being destructive simply because they can and they have the opportunity. And where anxiety really is the culprit, in about one-third of cases a change of diet will be enormously helpful, as many such dogs have food allergies or are sensitive to particular foods or ingredients. Some hyperactive dogs may simply be affected by high-protein diets. Many dogs may also find relief from alternative medicine and therapies as well.

In most cases destructive behaviour can be modified or eliminated through training, as there is nothing chemically wrong with the majority of dogs that behave in this way, distressed though they may seem. Here is a comprehensive list of causes of destructive behaviour that are *falsely* attributed to clinical anxiety:

• Exploratory behaviour and teething
• Lack of understanding of the right things to chew
• Sexual frustration
• Boredom
• Excess energy
• Barrier frustration – for instance, dislike of being locked up
• Competition with other dogs/animals/people in the house – for instance, urinating in the house
• Food stealing and/or bin raiding
• Redirected aggression – for instance, defecating around letterbox or windows
• Over-bonding or extreme attachment to a person or another animal
• Insufficient social contact with owner or machines (motorcycles, lawnmowers, etc.) and inside the house (fridge, TV, etc.)
• Pain and/or illness.

The most common separation-related problems are:

Barking while you're out of the house. Dogs bark – that's just what they do. But it isn't desirable if it is disturbing your neighbours, and so we must find ways to stop them from doing it.

Destructive behaviour. Puppies, of course, are very destructive, as teething and chewing are all part of their learning and development. It's important right from the beginning to give them 'legal' items to chew and to inform them when they have started on something 'illegal', such as a table leg or your shoes. When you're trying to train an older dog not to chew particular items or dig up things in your garden while you're away from home, you may need to look at other management solutions as well.

Soiling in the house. This very common and unfortunate problem often arises from competition with another dog in the household, or from separation issues or illness. The majority of dogs 'making mistakes' in the house, however, are doing it because they have been misinformed about where the right place is to eliminate, irrespective of opportunity in a proper environment. Fortunately, it is curable and manageable.

Below is an assortment of tried-and-tested ways to tackle separation-related problems.

• Make sure your dog gets enough exercise before you leave him alone. If excess energy is the problem and you'll be leaving him by himself for a time, you may need to go home to walk him during the day or use the dog-walking services of a friend, neighbour or a professional.

It's also unfair to expect a dog to control his bladder or bowels for many hours. They can do it, but they will suffer, just as you and I will. Always take your dog out to do his business *before* you leave him alone for a length of time.

• Try not to display any signs of going away, like putting on your business suit, applying make-up, hunting for your keys at the very beginning of getting ready – any of these may be pre-conditioned signals that will cause your dog distress. Whether you realise it or not, your leaving routine is just that: routine. Your dog knows when you're getting ready to leave him, as he sees you do it every day.

• Get your dog settled before you leave. You can tell him, 'Go to bed', and give him a treat when he does so. You can leave on a radio playing soft soothing music, or a TV. The gentle murmurings may just be enough to relax him. Or it may be that he will find an article of your clothing, like an old sweatshirt, comforting. If so, leave it with him in his bed.

• Don't make a big deal out of leaving the house. Some of us do this because we feel so guilty about having to leave our dogs behind. If you display lots of sympathetic gestures, use a sad voice and/or hug and kiss him a lot before you leave, you may be adding to his distress. Instead, give him a cheery 'Ciao!' and be on your way.

• If your dog is directing his chewing at a particular item when you aren't there to inform him that his behaviour is undesirable, don't allow him access to that item! If he likes to chew chair legs when you leave the house, don't let him be in a room with any chairs. Furthermore, leave him something that he is allowed to chew on, so that he has an outlet for his energy.

• If you're leaving your dog indoors when you go away, he may bark, chew things and eliminate, because he feels claustrophobic. Installing a dog flap in a door with direct excess to a proven dog-safe and protected garden may relieve the tension that is causing these unwanted behaviours.

• Alternatively, if you already have your dog outside or he is free to roam the house and he barks, he may have to be brought inside and confined to a safe and comfortable place. Guarding a garden or a house may be proving too much of a responsibility for him. Instead, he may need to be contained. Try a room, like the kitchen, or even a travel kennel (see Management solutions, p. 192).

• Interactive toys, long-lasting chews, a feeder on a timer, various objects stuffed with treats or dog food, together with a variety of feeding routines (for instance, scattering food around the garden), will keep your pet tired both physically and mentally. You'll also enjoy having a happy dog who can solve various tasks that have been authorised and encouraged by you. In addition to these toys, chews and games, there will soon be auto-training devices on the market that will help you to reinforce and promote many of your dog's good habits – settling down, staying quite, keeping to one side – without your having to be there.

Finally, good training will always come to your rescue, no matter what issues you have with your dog. He needs to know his social status and the rules of your household, as well as your preferences. He'll benefit from a good measure of structure and discipline. Equip yourself with as many skills as you can and you can Hand Feed (see p. 71) him to obedience.

There are many other common behavioural problems, and if you're plagued by any of the following you've not yet established a strong communication between yourself and your dog. You need to do some good solid training with him (and to work on yourself) to cement your position as his guide and leader and to solidify his entire dependency on you. If you're having behavioural problems with your dog, go back and work carefully through the Hand Feeding programme.

Fussy eating
'Molly, my collie-cross, is a finicky eater and often doesn't eat her dinner. Is there something wrong with her?'

Molly should first be checked by a vet before the start of any training or reconditioning aimed at making her eat properly, in order to make sure there is nothing medically amiss. If she passes her health exam and is in good condition – weight and activity-level wise – she will be ready for some training.

As we said earlier, most finicky eaters are perfectly healthy dogs that have learned that there will always be food around whenever they want it. They certainly get what they need nutritionally and are in no way underfed, but their philosophy becomes: 'No, I don't like this, and I won't touch that.' There is no doubt that this will affect not only a dog's eating habits but also many other issues, including his obedience training.

If you're leaving your dog's food out all day, there will be little reason for him ever to be ravenous. If you're doing this and your dog is fussy, just think about the reason why. Think about who he is. He is a dog that has the instincts to survive on his own. Not only can he survive, he *wants* to. This applies to domesticated dogs as well as wild dogs. The instinct is still there. There isn't much of a challenge if his food is always available, and he becomes blasé about eating.

Furthermore, by leaving your dog's dinner out all day, you've crowned him, unwittingly, king of the household. As we saw earlier, in the wild only the lead dog has the privilege of feeding at his leisure.

If you're only placing his food down at the appointed mealtime and he is still not eating, it is likely that either you're feeding him more than he requires or you're feeding him snacks during the day to compensate for his not eating his last meal. If your dog is healthy, I recommend that you begin immediately on my Hand Feeding programme (see p. 71), because if he is fussy, this is one of the tell-tale signs that you, my friend, are being held hostage by your dog. His finicky behaviour will soon dissolve as he learns that you're in charge of his food and are therefore his sole provider.

As long as your dog is getting the proper amount of food a day for his size and breed, it doesn't really matter if he's fed once, twice or five times a day, as long as he has learned that the food isn't free; it comes with conditions. See Chapter 4 for a systematic guide to proper eating habits and learning how to get your dog to look to you for guidance.

There is another useful measure that you can use after graduating in the Hand Feeding method. And your dog doesn't have to be fussy to enjoy it. Appealing to his desire to hunt, you can put his meal in devices such as an Activity Ball, training cube, or even an old sock, so that he literally has to work for his food. You might even consider hiding his meal, so that he has to hunt it down to eat it. Make sure that, whatever you use, you don't make it too hard for him at first, as you don't want him to give up and walk away.

Ari awaits a visitor.

If tomorrow you're going to go to your training class and tell the instructor, 'My dog is really not into food' or, 'He's not food-motivated', then read this advice on fussy eating again and again. This is probably the worst dog (or rather owner) behavioural problem that I have to deal with. It is harder to change than any other problem, even aggression. Hand Feeding is where you must start to change both your and your dog's attitude in order to promote his dependency on you.

Food obsession

'My pointer, Plato, is food-obsessed and is constantly getting into the bin or ruining people's picnics. What do I do?'

There is nothing wrong with a dog being keen on food. It is perfectly natural, and is in fact a desirable trait, as food is a great motivator in training. I would first determine whether or not Plato is getting the proper amount of a complete food on a daily basis. If he is, most likely his problem (again, I should strictly say his owner's) is that he hasn't been given a set of boundaries for his behaviour. Plato hasn't learned properly that he isn't supposed to scavenge in the bin or invade picnics.

Let's start with the bin problem. The management solution would be to move or block off the bin so that the dog has no access to it. If you want to leave the bin where it is, then your dog should not be given admittance to the room where it is without your being present. However, if you want to train him simply not to go into the bin, then you have several options. If he is so food-obsessed that he'll even go for the bin when you're standing right there in front of him, you can use one of your selected corrections, like spraying water on him or rattling a can. You could also put him on the lead and when he goes towards the bin, check him slightly. At the same time, you must begin rewarding him for not going to the bin. Ask him to sit, for instance. When he does, reward him. Remember that using positive reinforcement is the best way to help train away your dog's behavioural problems.

If your dog only raids the bin when you're out of the room, you'll need to be craftier. Try placing something on top of the lid, like a plastic bottle filled with pebbles, so that when he nudges the bin it will fall over and make a loud, aversive sound (this will only work properly if the object was introduced first as an aversion marker). Use your imagination, but whatever you use, make sure it won't harm your dog, only startle him.

Furthermore, you may need not only to be persistent with your tactics, but also to make sure that you first try out these experiments when you haven't really left the house but have only pretended. Or you could leave the house for a minute, then return to check if your dog has gone for the bin, and reset your distraction if necessary. The more determined your dog, the more subterfuge you'll require.

As for Plato's talent for crashing picnics uninvited, the same logic applies. When you're going out for walks, you must be alert to other people sitting on the ground eating. You must anticipate your dog's behaviour so that you'll be prepared to deal with it and correct his behaviour – or, much better, make sure he doesn't misbehave in the first place.

The management solution is either to simply to hook your dog back on the lead *before* you see picnickers (that is, when you're in a place where can expect to see some eventually) or leave him permanently on the lead. In the first instance, you'll have to be faster than your dog at spotting them. The second solution is much less satisfactory for most owners, as it's great to be able to let your dog off the lead, if legally permitted, to have a good run.

A better solution is to train your dog not to approach the picnickers. Place him on a long line. When you spot the picnic, begin to ask your dog to do other things like walking to heel, motivating him with titbits as you do. If your dog still heads in the picnicker' direction, step on the line, or pick it up, to give him a mild reminder. Ask him to follow some other direction, like 'sit'. When he does, reward him. In this way you're praising your dog when he is doing something right and correcting when he isn't. Try to remain calm, as your mood will influence the results of your training, not just here but always.

As you persist in this exercise, over time the lure of the picnickers will eventually be conditioned out of your dog's psyche because you're giving him a happy alternative: following your lead and being rewarded for it.

As we said above in connection with fussy eating, there are a couple of devices that allow dogs to literally hunt for their food. Food-obsessed dogs may just need a good challenge. In the case of a dog like Plato, when he is left alone in a room with the tempting bin, you can offer him an alternative: a Kong toy, an Activity Ball or a training ball filled with his meal. And it's legal! He can spend several happy hours trying to scavenge for his food, forgetting about the bin entirely. In conjunction with the other methods listed above, such devices are certainly worth exploring. Just remember to put them at first on settings that aren't too hard. Otherwise your dog might give up and head for the bin – an easier target.

Hyperactivity at mealtime

'My rescue dog, Sam, is playing up at mealtime. The mere smell of food sends him into a frenzy. What's wrong with him?'

This kind of behaviour isn't unusual. I've seen dozens of oddities that dogs display at feeding time, including one long-haired miniature dachshund, Gretchen, who spins in dizzying circles and barks while her meal is being prepared – every single time without fail.

Sam's behaviour really shouldn't surprise us and there isn't anything wrong with it in itself, as we want our dogs to be food-dependent and therefore excited in anticipation of it. Remember, in the wild, scavenging and hunting for food takes up most of a dog's time. In their domestic domain, there may be little else to get them as excited as eating.

So, if your dog does find this time inordinately thrilling, why not give him a challenge and go with his nature? As mentioned in the case studies on fussy eating and food obsession (pp. 203 and 205), some exceptional products are available at all good pet shops and have given many hyper dogs relief: the Kong toy, Buster Cube and Activity Ball. At mealtime you fill the device with his dinner (apart from the Kong, which only works with dry food) and set it down for him. Each of these items has an opening from which food is dispensed when the dog pushes the object around.

It's also worth exploring the tactic of ignoring your dog in this instance. In this way you may break the connection between the food being prepared or measured and its being delivered. Not knowing when to expect the meal, the dog will learn to wait attentively and patiently settle to wait until you're ready to feed him.

Pulling on the lead

'My Weimaraner is pulling like mad on the lead. Winnie acts like a yo-yo and keeps tripping me up. How can I get him to walk well?'

Why do dogs pull on the lead? Because they can. Sometimes continuously, sometimes only once in a while. They choose to pull in order to investigate, hunt or simply to help you walk. They may prefer to lead rather than to follow. They make up their own rules. Little pups especially will be trying out their boundaries and zigzagging everywhere just to see what happens – not challenging you or testing you, but just because they enjoy it. It may even have little or nothing to do with how they feel about their status and everything to do with what they've learned from the very beginning about being on the lead. If your dog is pulling, he hasn't learned what he needs to accomplish this exercise correctly.

Whether your dog is an adult or a new pup, you're going to have to successfully learn how to direct his attention towards you. He needs to be conditioned to look to you for guidance, especially on walks both on and off the lead. Here the Hand Feeding method (see p. 71) is again useful, as this is exactly what it will achieve. Once this task has been accomplished, everything else is much easier to learn or relearn properly.

Like all behavioural issues, walking properly on the lead isn't an isolated issue, it is one that I feel is part of your dog's education. Just as we need basic maths before we can learn calculus, our dogs need to learn several basic skills and be conditioned to look to us for guidance before they can walk to heel properly.

If you have problems with your dog on the lead, I can guarantee you also have other issues to work on with him. This is so even if you might not admit it or recognise the issues as problems; some people don't think of it as problematic, for instance, that their dog comes back *eventually* instead of right away when called. So go back to Hand Feeding and basic commands (p. 71) to teach yourself and your dog the basic required attitude.

To tackle the problem of pulling on the lead, many people use the quickest and cheapest way to manage the problem – ceasing to walk their dog on the lead. No lead, no pulling. But I can't put my support 100% behind this management solution because you have to think of the safety of your dog. According to a survey conducted by Battersea Dogs' Home, nearly one in five people are prepared to put their dogs and others at risk by not keeping their dogs on the lead when walking on or near roads, side streets and car parks. There is always a risk that even the best-trained dog can be startled, attacked, spooked, or will just run off, and possibly be injured or killed. Why take that chance?

Every time your dog pulls, you have a few options at your disposal, as described below, all of which you can use individually or together. Whatever you decide to use, I suggest you feed him all through his first few walks until you've conditioned him to understand that a good walk means food. Later you can begin to introduce the concept of no nice walking, no food. In this way you start off on a positive note, the best way of all.

In addition, you can use these traditional solutions:

1. Give your dog a *gentle* check on the lead and keep doing it every single time for as long as it takes him to get the message that pulling means trouble. Every time he doesn't pull but instead chooses to walk by your side, reward him. It takes owners a long time to master holding the end of a 3–4-foot lead and keeping it slack during these good moments, but this approach doesn't work without it.

2. Every time your dog pulls, turn around and head back in the opposite direction to the one he wants to go in, until he is walking neatly by your side. Then turn around again and head back in the direction that you want to take. Treat him when he does walk by your side.

3. When your dog begins to pull, return home and hang up the lead. Wait ten minutes and try again. Granted, this is a cumbersome technique

but it will prove very effective if you have the stamina to adhere to it religiously. In this vein, there are many other techniques that can be categorised as negative stimuli, punishment or reprimand. To give just two, you can squirt him with water or keep dropping the lead.

4. Using Hand Feeding, you can deliver your dog's breakfast to him while walking – one biscuit every two steps or one small handful every ten. Where's he going to be if he wants his food? And how much food will he get if he's not right by your side? All of this, of course, is just a friendly recap for you. You know what to do – it's now time to apply it.

Jody, RSPCA rescue German Shepherd
has settled beautifully into his new life.

The most important thing to remember is *consistency*. Your dog will never learn how to walk properly on the lead if today you correct him for pulling on the lead, tomorrow you don't, next Tuesday you do, and the week after that you're too busy talking with your walking companion to notice what your dog is doing. This applies to all of your training. You can't reward him for good behaviour sometimes and then not at all at other times. You have to target the problem, stay focused and, in the beginning, work at it *every time and all the time.*

Teaching an adult dog how to walk well on the lead is, admittedly, challenging, and my methods aren't overnight quick fixes but require time and energy if you want your dog to understand that he shouldn't pull. But I do appreciate that not everyone has the time required to pursue training to its fullest impact.

Happily, modern technology has given us some very helpful training aids that can speed up the process, or at least prevent the unwanted activity from occurring if not actually teaching the dog anything. They aren't my ideal choice, but they may be right for you. Using them should be no admission of failure, as we all have to do what we can in the time we're willing to dedicate to a problem. And why shouldn't we be able to use all the tools available to us?

As mentioned earlier, there are several products that dog owners have used with success, like Halti and Gentle Leader head collars, and body harnesses (p. 195). Whatever you choose, back it up with rewards. When your dog ceases to pull on the lead, reward him for his good behaviour with a steady and ample supply of treats. For although he may be prevented from pulling against his will, he'll be learning that staying by your side is a positive and rewarding move.

Jumping up on people

'Benji, my Labrador, gives everyone a wonderful welcome when they arrive. He likes to place his paws right on their shoulders and lick their faces. While I find this adorable, most of my visitors don't. How can I suppress this behaviour?'

This is a classic complaint and one that needs to be addressed, because few people, myself excluded, want to be on the receiving end of a dog, big or small, that slobbers on their cheeks and possibly makes their clothes dirty. Little dogs seem to get away with this behaviour more, simply because of their size. But in all cases it's terribly bad manners and will do little to endear you to others.

The way to solve this problem is to inform your dog that jumping up on people is unwanted and that not jumping on people is nice, and to motivate him to choose the latter. Clear and consistent communication is your dearest friend in this game. Try placing a saucer or dish with a few biscuits on a table by your front door and you'll soon be well on your way to training the Pavlovian way: the doorbell rings, the dog begins to salivate, a person appears at the front door, your dog sits, and then he gets a treat. An effective Hand Feeding solution.

It's critical to reward your dog's good behaviour, however slight it may be at the start. Every time your dog *doesn't* jump on a new arrival at your door, give him a treat and tell him how good he is. If you don't, he won't know what to replace his jumping behaviour with and you won't be encouraging him in a new and positive direction.

Running off and insistent recall

'My Tibetan spaniel, Cuba, is very good at home and quite obedient off the lead, but there are times when I can't get him back. Why is he obedient at home but not outside?'

If you're reading this section because your dog runs off and doesn't come back when called – at least not right away – congratulations! Admitting you have a problem is half the battle. And you aren't alone. There are thousands of Cubas running away and not coming back when called. Luckily, though, Cuba's problem is easily solved as he already walks well with you.

A dog like Cuba hasn't understood that when you tell him to stay, he must not run off after that lovely ginger cat; and that when you ask him to come to you, he will, no matter what else is going on around him. You can't expect a dog to be perfectly trained if he hasn't been given the appropriate knowledge, as well as educated through reinforcement and use of distractions.

Dogs that have been through the Hand Feeding programme don't suffer from this disorder. Tell me, who would want to run off when all you have to do to obtain your breakfast is to go for a walk with your handler while your food is dispensed every few minutes – near every park bench, or after every recall? You miss one, and you're out of luck. You'd want to stick around too!

There is no alternative way for a dog to feed unless he becomes a very successful hunter. But why should he when he can rely on you and your instructions and challenges and look to you for his sustenance? I know two standard poodles, Porsha and Mitsi, who live together and discovered the benefits of staying close to their owners through Hand Feeding. In fact, they stayed so close that their owners wanted to know how to get them to run further afield. After only six or seven private sessions, we had successfully replaced their hunting and disappearing habits with playing rough and tumble, jumping up at their owners – they like it, so that's OK – looking up for their next instructions and doing lots of sits, stays and emergency stops. Do they have enough exercise now that they aren't flying through the woods? Absolutely. They come home after their walkies and collapse with exhaustion from all the new, unexpected and unpredictable experiences that their owners are providing. Porsha and Mitsi are typical examples, not exceptional at all in their behaviour. Why would they want to rush off from their handlers when life is so good if they stay close? But it does take time and effort to achieve such results, and you may benefit from the following tips.

Put your dog on a long line – not a retractable lead, as these can actually encourage pulling – when you're outside walking. That way, when he doesn't return to you when prompted, you can deliver a correction – check him back gently with the lead or simply cut out the option of his succeeding at it. If you're letting the lead just drag along the ground, you can step on it, which gives him a correction if he tries to run off in another direction. Often, however, the mere existence of the lead attached to the dog – whether or not you're holding the other end – can convince him to stick around, and he may not even attempt to run off. A correction may never be necessary.

In using a long lead you have the luxury of correcting your dog at a distance. You can make a lead as long as you like. Thirty-foot leads are sold and I've found this to be the optimal length, but you can tie leads together to make one as long as you like. You can also use a long piece of rope, available from most hardware stores. Just remember to use it safely, and be careful of people around you.

And don't forget that when your dog does come back to you when requested, make a big deal out of it! The key is to both motivate him to want to come back to you and to correct him when he doesn't. The following story will give you more insight into this issue and how to handle a not-so-perfect dog, or one with baggage. Commitment and a positive approach, coupled with the appropriate knowledge, will get you the results you want.

Doushman and Kasbek playing together in the surf.

SKY

Sky is a beautiful and gentle Samoyed, but, true to her breed, she's very independent. She would take herself off for long walks, four or five hours at a stretch, leaving her walker or owner way behind. Sky was walked by a professional dog walker – a lovely lady with a sweet nature – for three and half years. But Sky abused her trust and that of her owner, even running out of the house before she could be taken for a walk. A matter of discipline and control? It was more of a case of the 'Let me catch my dog and I'll show you how obedient she is!' syndrome. Whether it was a case of the dog walker giving up or the owners having had enough of Sky's antics, one day I found Sky and her young family standing in front of me ready to start training.

I advise all my trainees to attend my classes for a full 15-week course, where they will learn new approaches and techniques every time with me, and to practise at home with their dogs in between. During this time I can educate both parties on most training issues. Sky came to see me once a week accompanied by one of her family members, James or Laura. They both worked during the day but practised with Sky together to keep each other informed of new developments.

Step by step, they all learned what to do, how to listen, how to ask for and get things, and how to earn rewards. It gradually became easier for Sky, as she started to look forward to being trained and easily cracked new challenges one after the other – distractions, temptations and new horizons of the human-dog companion relationship. She even began to work with toys and other dogs to replace her escapism, much to everyone's delight. In a few months Sky and her family graduated from the Good Boy Dog School fully equipped with enough knowledge and ideology to continue to live and apply their learning on their own.

It has been about three years since Sky graduated from my school and I believe she has had only one ten-minute escape from her walker. Other than this one transgression, she always comes and stays with her and goes on long off-lead walks in many parks and open spaces. Sky is a happy and relaxed dog, assured by the love and commitment of her family and of anyone who exercises her for them. Exactly how it is meant to be.

Not paying attention

'My Rottweiler loves treats, but when he sees other dogs, Jay ignores the treats I'm offering and runs after them, not listening to me. What can I do?'

Jay hasn't finished his training, although his owner has done well as Jay responds to food training and is happy to work for her in normal circumstances. But he needs to learn to follow his handler's lead even when there are great doggie distractions.

It isn't enough to teach your dog basic obedience commands. These must also be reinforced through distraction training (see p. 147). Many people take training classes indoors that are nearly devoid of normal outside stimuli. Is it any wonder that a dog that will sit when asked to do so in the kitchen doesn't do it when he's outside and a motorbike zooms past?

Attention seeking

'Alfi, my Weimaraner, whines incessantly every time he wants something, from biscuits to going out for his walkies – whether it's time to go or not. It drives me crazy! Is there anything I can do to stop this annoying habit?'

Clearly, Alfi is a very effective communicator! He has figured out what gets his owner's attention, and because he continues to do it, I can only surmise that the owner is doing as Alfi is requesting in order to restore peace and quiet. But the more you acquiesce in such a situation, the more a dog will persist in his behaviour.

If your dog is like Alfi, start informing him about your views on what is allowed and not allowed in the house. You also need a lesson on leadership from Gentle leaders versus dictators (p. 178) and perhaps Corrections (p. 129). You need to gain control and learn how to instruct him that his whining is undesirable and, instead, that maintaining silence is nice behaviour. With a little persistence and knowledge, you can nip this issue in the bud quickly and effectively. Otherwise, your dog will have you granting his every whim and as your reward you'll be an unpaid butler!

Barking at passers-by, cars, cyclists and motorcyclists

'Every time someone walks by our house, Willy and Wiley, my two Jack Russell terriers, bark from the living room window. The neighbours are complaining. What can I do to make them stop?'

This is annoying, is often perceived as aggression and is a nuisance. Don't allow your dogs to do it. But how do you stop it even after you've tried all the management solutions – like shutting the curtains or making the front rooms inaccessible, so that they can't see people?

First, condition your dogs to like the time someone is outside. 'Oh look, there's a neighbour out there. Isn't that nice? Here's a treat – oh, have another – you've been so good.' (They can't eat and bark at the same time, can they?) Divert them with 'Sit', 'Go to bed', 'Down' or 'Beg' each time they see a passer-by. Treat and reward them only when they have been successful. Give them a choice: meal or bark.

Car drama
'Dogs feel very strongly that they should always go with you in the car, in case the need should arise for them to bark violently at nothing right in your ear.' **Dave Barry**

If I had to pick the most annoying dog behaviour, it's this one. There is nothing worse than trying to drive, find your way around and concentrate while you have a nutcase in the car barking or whining in your ear and jumping from left to right, forward and back. My clients complain that this behaviour is right up there with screaming children in the back seat as one of their least favourite things in life.

There are two main instances where dogs behave badly in cars. Either they are uneasy with cars or they get too excited about them. In either case they were never instructed how to behave properly.

In addition to re-educating your dog first through Hand Feeding (see p. 71), which teaches him to be respectful and mindful, there are a variety of further solutions.

If you feel your dog is simply terrified of the car, you need to show him that it is a safe and fun place to be. Train him just as you would in travel-kennel training (see Management solutions, p. 192). Show him that the car is a safe and comforting place. You can even use the kennel in the car. Treats, toys and praise will go a long way here, but you mustn't *push* your dog into the car mentally or physically. He has to go in happily on his own. Hand Feeding, every step of the way from the house to into the car, will condition the whole event as a comfortable experience for him. Take your time, but if you haven't mastered it in a week, you may need help as you could be doing something wrong. Even the best trainers need someone to look over their shoulder once in a while.

You can also try to desensitise your dog's feeling about the car. Spend some time just sitting inside it with him, without the engine running. When he is comfortable doing this – and it may take a few sessions – you can graduate to turning the engine on but still not moving. Again, allow your dog to get comfortable with this. You too need to sit back and relax, and demonstrate that you aren't stressed by the experience, either. Only when your dog has been acting consistently well should you attempt to go for a short ride. Drive just a few yards, or around the block at most. Return home and praise him lavishly for his good behaviour. Gradually you'll be able to build him up to longer rides. Try driving somewhere that's rewarding for him, like the park. Or, every time you reach your destination, give him a jackpot of rewards and praise. You'll soon have a dog that can't wait to get in the car.

A time-consuming but often effective measure for the overexcited dog is to enlist the help of another person (someone has to drive the car, after all, and have both hands on the wheel), so that you can use the standard practice of *informing* your dog of what is expected of him and *motivating* him to do it while you're driving around. However, if you haven't a pal to help you out, you can teach your dog yourself. Try the following.

Get in your car and put your dog in the back seat. Sit in front, behind the wheel, where you'd normally be. Don't turn on the engine. Ignore your dog. Read a magazine if you like – this could take a while.

Don't allow your dog to jump into the passenger seat or on to you. Keep rewarding him for not doing so every now and then, but if he succeeds, send him back to the back seat. You want to teach him that there are boundaries and that he must respect them – always. Your job is to drive, his job is to wait politely in the back seat or right in the back (in the case of SUVs and estate cars) until you've reached your destination. Don't wait until his patience expires; treat him for good behaviour, no matter how small it may seem.

Beagle bedtime.

If after you've practised positively motivating him for some weeks, your dog begins to bark or whine, remove him from the car and put him back in the house. Try again ten minutes later. You may have to do this several times before he begins to settle down. But you didn't expect to solve the problem overnight, did you? Practice makes perfect, as always.

When you're finally successful in getting your dog to be calm and quiet in the car, reward him and tell him what a good boy he is. Then turn on the engine and sit there. This gives you the opportunity again to praise your dog when he's acting well and to use a correction when necessary. Try this for ten minutes a day until you feel satisfied that he is ready to take a ride.

If, when you finally do begin to drive around, your dog acts up again, either stop or drive straight back home and put him indoors. Go out and do your errands without him. Try the exercise later or the next day. Eventually he'll get the message that only when he behaves will the car take him to the park for fun.

There are some practical training aids and management tools you can employ to stop manic car behaviour. If your dog is simply overexcited and bounds around the car, contain him by using a barrier across the back seat that confines him to the back of the car (dog guards come as standard for most car models today, but you can also get them at car accessory stores) or put him in a travel kennel.

You may also manage him with a short lead, a chain or a car harness that restrains him to a spot in the car. I believe it will one day become law to have your dog safely restrained, just as it is for children. You may also try to concoct a strategy that will require him to concentrate on his meal in the back of the car. A food-filled Kong toy, for instance, may just last the length of your journey, keeping him occupied all the way.

As explained earlier, if your dog barks you can invest in a citronella bark collar (p. 196), which emits a burst of citronella near his face when he barks. It's triggered by a built-in mechanism that will correct him as required, leaving you free to reward him when he is behaving well. (Why haven't they come up with a self-rewarding collar? It would come in handy for this kind of situation.)

Situational fears

'My rescue dog is afraid of going to the vet. Horace shakes, barks, and fidgets, making it nearly impossible for him to be examined properly. I don't want to medicate him. Is there anything else I can do?'

Horace isn't alone. There are lots of common fears that dogs have: going to the vet or groomer, thunderstorms, fireworks and the noise of the vacuum cleaner, to list just a few. These are all learned fears and, one way or another, you or someone else probably helped unwittingly to foster or encourage them. So, if a dog has been conditioned to fear something, logic suggests that he can be conditioned eventually out of it. It just takes some initiative and persistence.

One of our star Good Boy Dog School graduates is a regal white lurcher named Casper. His story will shed some light on what it takes to overcome fears and phobias.

CASPER

Casper was rescued at the age of one from Battersea Dogs' Home by Barbara, who quickly discovered that he had no skills whatsoever, either indoors or out. He was also claustrophobic, scared of other dogs and of walking along the road, as well as of going to the vet. Barbara had her work cut out for her and she tackled one problem at a time, basic obedience being her first step. She taught Casper that there was no free lunch. He had to work for every treat. Barbara was intensely diligent and her considerable efforts paid off. Only when she had conquered Casper's obedience problem did she embark on solving his fears of the vet. Her solution worked brilliantly.

Barbara had trained Casper using a clicker and she relied heavily on this in tackling his vet fear as it gave him an alternative focus and a crutch to lean on. She also told the vet's office staff what she was doing and gained their support. At first, she began walking Casper near the vet's premises, all the while putting him through his paces and his obedience routine. She clicked and treated him as they went along, putting certain things on cue – turning away from some people, passing by dogs, doing sits, leaning against her while they walked to heel. She did this on several outings, gradually getting closer to the vet's until she could walk him to the door without issue.

She followed the same programme to get him to walk inside the door, never pushing him, but being patient and backing off if she felt Casper wasn't quite ready. She continued to encourage him by using the click and treat method. She also used a reward system of jackpots, where he was given a large amount of treats when he accomplished a major feat.

This same method got Casper in the door and sitting quietly inside, where he was given lots of attention and rewards, and finally in the vet's room for an examination. They had several mock visits with everyone clued into the charade and making the experience rewarding for Casper – all part of his positive reconditioning.

Now, instead of going into fits of fear at the sight of the vet's, he runs in happily. Is it any wonder? Casper has now learned that it's a nice place to go. It wasn't a fast process, but it was a rewarding solution. Barbara was able to communicate to Casper through encouragements and reward that his fears were unfounded. Every step took less effort to succeed as Casper began looking forward to new situation training games – which is how Casper and Barbara saw their work together.

Any dog's fears can be overcome with work and determination. Take it slowly, motivating your dog through rewards as he overcomes his fears one step at a time.

Aggression and biting
'Every dog isn't a growler, and every growler isn't a dog.'
Anonymous

I'm probably best known for my work with aggressive dogs. News of my success in my early work in Britain with dogs like Benson and Wolf quickly spread and I found myself being asked by the RSPCA and Battersea Dogs' Home to help specifically with difficult cases. I often get the dogs that are on death row – dogs that might have to be put down because they aren't re-homeable in their current state. Many dogs come to our school with the problem of aggression. When the problem gets really out of control, their owners, having had enough of their behaviour, realise that saving money on dog training isn't working.

Pain or illness, insecurity, possessiveness, timidity, lack of play and socialisation or 'bite-hibition', misreading other dogs' signals, protectiveness, being mistreated or provoked, feeling vulnerable or simply fighting back when attacked can all lead to what we think of as aggression. Many of my new clients regale me with stories about how their dogs only attack men with umbrellas, or people wearing black, or just dogs of a certain breed or gender. I've even come across dogs, although very rarely, who genuinely seem to like to fight.

In reality, what we call aggressive behaviour is exclusively learned behaviour. No matter, there is always one of the above underlying issues involved and wise owners of such dogs will seek professional assistance immediately before someone is injured.

I've always used a combination of elements to confront aggression in a dog. Hand Feeding (see p. 71), good and safe management, resocialisation and both positive and negative stimuli (see p. 29) are all needed. It takes time and patience. But it is something that can be overcome, first and foremost with the right commitment and love for the dog – no matter what his age or background. And if you aren't able in the end to solve the problem to your total satisfaction, be assured that the matter can be managed. It just requires focus, love and attention. *Remember, there are no bad dogs, just dogs that don't know how to behave properly.* It's up to you to teach them that there is an alternative – being good.

The following case studies examine the most common kinds of aggression and how to solve them.

Possessiveness

'No one is allowed to get near Lucky, my shih-tzu, when he is chewing on a bone. He will lunge at anyone within a ten-foot radius. We have children coming around for the holidays. Will Lucky have to be locked up for Christmas?'

I see this problem quite frequently. Dogs can act out when they are resting in a place they feel is their own, anywhere from their own bed to your bed, to under the dining table. They can also display possessiveness over items such as toys and bones, as in Lucky's case.

Dogs act possessively simply because they don't understand sharing space or objects with others, they benefit from acting this way and they are permitted to do so. As your dog's leader and guide, as the occupant of your house, you should be able to do anything you wish in it. If you want to sit in your dog's bed, he should have no issue with it. If you want to take a bone from his mouth, you should be able to. If you want to put your nose right up to his feeding bowl while he's eating it, that is your right. This is all achievable if you go along with the Hand Feeding regime, as we try to cover every step on the way towards eliminating bad behaviour completely, or even preventing it from happening in the first place.

Besides your dog learning through Hand Feeding that he is both food-dependent and dependent on you for his food, and learning that you're his teacher, leader and friend, you may find that a management solution may alleviate your concerns for good. As you're aware of the occasions when your dog acts possessively, you'll be able to anticipate his behaviour and be prepared for it. Although none of my own dogs has ever demonstrated aggressive tendencies towards me, this is a common complaint among my new trainees, and I see it too, sometimes in the lodgers that stay with me.

Every time your dog snarls he is sending you the message that he hasn't yet learned the basics of training successfully. Being protective is the same as being ignorant. He has to learn that he has nothing to gain from acting this way, only the loss of comfort and nutrients. But the moment he hesitates or is on the edge of snapping, that's the time to reward him with treats and praise, defusing the situation. The use of a negative stimulus may help you win the dispute, but if not, you must win anyway, or the results could be tragic one day, if not today. Then, as your dog improves and he chooses not to snarl or bite at you when you approach, reward him with a treat or a game with his favourite toy.

You let your dog win by losing, and you make him lose by your trying to win.

Anxiety around children

Doushman the Afghan gives a friendly smile.

'Is it worth taking the risk of introducing my dog to children, when she seems to be scared of them? We don't have any children of our own, but some of our friends do, and we'd like to be able to have their children come for a visit.'

This is a very good question and the solution requires great care and consideration on your part. I would never recommend experimenting on anyone's children (or adults) whether they be part of your family or not. Dogs that are anxious around children can snap, and that is the last thing you want.

Sidney and Coleman have been properly socialised
to live happily with children.

There are several ways to tackle the problem, depending on your particular situation and the age of the children. You may decide that the problem is much better managed by either keeping your dog separated from the children at all times or having him wear a muzzle in their company (see Using a muzzle, p. 234). This is always the advice I give to owners of older aggressive dogs. A management solution is the safest option in this instance.

If the children are infants, you can protect them by keeping your dog on the lead and, at the same time, encouraging a happy, stress-free environment by rewarding him for his good behaviour. If every time children come to your home, your dog has a positive experience, then his anxiety about children will eventually decrease and he will look on their visit as a happy time. This requires a steady, guaranteed frequency of positive experiences.

If the children are old enough to join in the training, that will make it even better. Any amount of positive emotions you can bring into the relationship between your dog and the children will only be beneficial. But dog training around toddlers is a difficult task, as children this young don't yet understand how their boundless energy can affect a nervous dog, and, of course, they are also on the move, which makes it hard to protect them. In this instance I must recommend separating the children from the dog. But try to make this a positive experience too, so that your dog doesn't feel reprimanded for something he hasn't even done. You can try clicker training, for instance. Using the same techniques as in 'send away' or obstacle training, every time he looks at a child, click and treat him. A child walks by while you're out for a walk – click and treat.

Dog-against-dog aggression

'The more I socialise my collie, the more she seems to be frightened of other dogs and attempts to attack them. Why doesn't Bijou like other dogs? What can I do?'

It is quite true that some dogs don't want the company of other dogs, whether this be learned or just part of their nature. But why doesn't Bijou just ignore other dogs? The fact that she is actually becoming aggressive is a sign that something else is amiss and it probably has to do in part with her owner's increasing anxiety. Whether the owner knows it or not, her unease is being transferred to Bijou and she is acting up.

Furthermore, just because you're taking your dog out to socialise doesn't mean that she is being socialised correctly. Good socialisation skills are learned within the first three months of a pup's life, or soon after, and that is probably when Bijou learned to compensate for her uncertainty and to strike first. It's hard to catch up after this time, but it is possible, as I manage such dogs all the time. (See Step 4: Active Socialisation Under Supervision (p. 153) for ways to manage unsociable dogs.)

Dog-against-human aggression

'My Dalmatian, Max, hates all visitors, although he is fine with humans outside as they never get that close. I try to soothe him when he barks when people enter the house, but I can't calm him down. He hasn't bitten anyone, yet, but I fear it is only a matter of time.'

Dogs are aggressive towards humans because they haven't been taught to act otherwise. And in some cases, like Max's, their aggression may have been encouraged. A dog that is misbehaving as badly as Max should not be getting positive attention from his owner for his aggression. Instead, Max should be informed that his behaviour is unwanted. Soothing him is only encouraging him, sending him a message that what he is doing is right. However, when he is acting properly, Max needs to be rewarded so that he learns what he should be doing instead – greeting humans that enter his house with a calm and warm welcome. (See Hand feeding by others, p. 128, Corrections, p. 129, and Socialisation, p. 153.) If Max is asked to sit when visitors enter the house and he is given a consistent jackpot of rewards for his compliance, he'll quickly learn that being attentive to his owner (or visitors, if they have the rewards) is more rewarding than barking at guests. Attaching positive associations to people – whether visitors or passers-by – is the best training method to rapidly change Max's reactions from aggressive to welcoming.

On-lead aggression

'My boxer, Lucy, is very docile and sweet, both indoors and out and is very friendly towards people and other dogs. But when I put her on the lead she becomes aggressive towards other dogs, barking and lunging. I need to walk her on the lead when we walk on the street, as I don't want her to run into the road. It's also the law. Is there anything I can do to prevent her from acting this way?'

This is a very common problem and one that, if not handled immediately, becomes a positively reinforced behaviour. In that case you have to address the aggression first. Reconditioning through desensitisation and resocialisation will go a long way towards tackling this issue.

However, on-lead aggression can be avoided or solved by looking at your body language, in particular how you're holding your lead, when you see another dog approaching. There is a handle at the end of the lead. The purpose of the handle is for you to hold it and to allow the lead to remain loose. 'LOOSE!' is the key word. If you bind the lead up, drawing your dog into your body to keep him close to you while other dogs are passing, you're restricting his freedom. Your dog will become very uncomfortable, perhaps feel vulnerable, and in many cases hostile.

At the same time, your body language is exascerbating his behaviour. You may become wary when you see another dog approaching, taking evasive measures. This only compounds the problem. So, not only should the lead be kept loose, so should you! Your fear will be transmitted, as if through an electric cable, through your hand, down the lead, right into your dog's mind. By alerting your dog to your fear, he'll only react accordingly in an antisocial way. What other choice are you giving him?

Dima and his students ready for a class.

On the other hand, when your dog manages to breezily walk by another dog without making a fuss, reward him jubilantly. In this way you'll be communicating the proper message to him. Here's what your dialogue should resemble: start communicating with your dog at a great distance away from the dog that is approaching. Reward your dog for each small success before he has a chance to act badly – be proactive, not reactive to his antics. Take another step forward. Still calm – good. 'Here's your biscuit. Oh, you want another one? Fine. Now sit [or stay]. Good boy!' Wait, and another reward. Loose lead and … what aggression? Put your dog through his obedience routine and before you know it, you've passed by the other dog without incident. It's all a matter of focus.

At a later stage you may need to choose a way to inform your dog that his aggressive behaviour isn't welcome. Trying halting, or making a sharp turn away with him. Experiment until you find what works for the two of you. But remember, reward your dog's good behaviour the second you see it. This can only encourage him in a positive direction.

Using a muzzle

It is wise to muzzle your dog if you're experiencing problems with him, at the very least until you have the problem solved. Back in Russia, dogs had to be muzzled as part of their general obedience test. This was an important practice. Although we weren't required to muzzle our dogs in general, it helped them to become accustomed to it, so if they did need to wear one, they would do so without making a fuss. It also kept them from picking up the bad habit of foraging and eating things they shouldn't.

Many people choose to muzzle their dogs not because their dogs are aggressive but because they don't want to take the slight chance that they might bite someone. That's OK. When I worked briefly in Germany, I met a gentleman with a German shepherd wearing a muzzle on the street. 'Is he aggressive?' I asked understandingly. 'No,' he replied, 'not that I know of – but I don't want to know!'

The dog obviously was used to it, and it gave his owner peace of mind. So why not? If you have any doubts, why take chances?

If you're unsure of your dog, a muzzle is a very wise acquisition. It's no admission of failure to insist that your dog wear one. It is a perfectly appropriate measure. Muzzles aren't particularly appreciated by the British public, but it is you who have to make choices and sacrifices for your dog, not anyone else.

Although I've never come across a dog that, after proper training, hasn't been successfully rehabilitated, I know that some dogs can't be completely cured of their aggressive tendencies. This can be because of the dog's character and nervous disposition or sometimes because the problem is so ingrained that the time required to solve it may be more than the owner wishes to give. But most often it's because the owner has reached the end of their learning or ambition and the dog has stalled at some point because of this. In addition, your past with your aggressive dog may cause you to never fully trust him; whether in reality you can or can't is beside the point. If you aren't comfortable and are unsure of your dog's aggression, I urge you not to take any chances and to have your dog wear a muzzle as one of the few ways to avoid and manage otherwise antisocial behaviour.

There are some people who, no matter how aggressive their dogs are, can't bring themselves to put a muzzle on their dog, thinking it's cruel. All I can say is shame on them for putting what is essentially only a mere inconvenience on their dogs – which would become routine in time for the dog and perfectly comfortable – above the safety of others. If you're debating whether or not to use a muzzle on your dog, the mere fact that you're thinking about it probably means you need to do it. Don't put it off any longer, but take responsibility for your dog now. Take time also to teach him to like his muzzle, conditioning this with treats. You'll be able to enjoy your walks, as you'll no longer have to worry about your dog harming a child, adult or another dog. And I'll wager that he'll feel better as well, because of your new-found calm and because once he realises that his lunging and attacking is getting him nowhere, he too can start to relax and enjoy himself.

Below are a few case studies to show you, primarily, that you aren't alone in having a dog that's difficult to manage, and that happy outcomes aren't just fantasy. As frustrating, dangerous and often embarrassing as the problem of aggression is, you can triumph over it through both training and attentive management.

One interesting case is Julia, my co-author's dog. Julia was nearly seven years of age when I met her and she had been displaying aggressive behaviour since she was seven months old. Why did Julia's owners let the problem fester for so long? There were the usual excuses, ranging from their inexperience with dog training, an unfortunate inability to find an appropriate trainer over the years despite their efforts, and the fact of moving so often that they never had the opportunity to confront the issue properly head-on with any consistency. They were amazingly fortunate not to have had any very serious incidents in this time. But, in the end, Emily resocialised Julia to remarkable effect. Their experience will help others, I'm sure.

JULIA

You may have to put up with questions about why your dog is muzzled, especially if it's a cute little Jack Russell like Julia. She is an adorable and dainty dog but with the fighting spirit of a lion. Never judge a book by its cover!

I first bumped into Emily on the Heath while I was walking my morning charges and she asked for my help. I'm very familiar with the antics of Jack Russells and therefore don't always buy into their sweet expressions or deceptively cute little faces (like their owners do). I know their true potential. When I first met Julia, I did wonder how far her 'I rule the Earth' self-image was established. I was not to be disappointed.

Learning about how a dog and owner communicate can be an interesting process, and sometimes it takes a while for all the problems to unfold and show themselves. Such was the case with Julia, who is – as all who know her appreciate – a bit of a stage actress. She can put on the charm when required. So, when we started I saw at the very beginning that it wasn't other dogs that Julia had an issue with – at least she seemed to get on with all the dogs we introduced her to in our group. Occasionally, though, she displayed a dislike for some people, lunged at a cat on someone's front lawn or tried to fly after a squirrel in the park.

Her basic obedience skills were there – or rather she knew *how* to sit or walk by Emily's side. Would she do this if you asked her? You'd have to be lucky to witness this particular miracle. Julia would turn and give her owner a bright little puppy smile, and Emily, completely smitten, would leave it at that, passing off her non-compliance as a terrier character trait. That was the extent of Emily's insistence on Julia's training.

I took Julia and Emily back to the beginning and started them on Hand Feeding, as I usually do to reverse this common attitude that both Julia and Emily portrayed. They needed to learn how to work together happily. They switched to their new routine without incident and all was proceeding nicely until the first walk we went out on together with other doggie pals and their owners. It was then that I saw Julia's true Dr Jekyll and Mr Hyde personality. After an hour and a half of socialising happily with many dogs – probably 30 or more – suddenly a new dog joined us and fur flew. The poor border terrier didn't know what hit him. I reacted quickly as we had both expected something like this to happen eventually, given Julia's chequered past. No damage was done, but the predicted did occur – not to anyone's surprise.

Julia needed masses of resocialisation with other dogs and Emily doled out tons of food on their walks together. Emily took her on daily hikes with me for a few months until she had the confidence to go it alone. Even then, Julia could be fine for weeks and then suddenly POW! She'd try to strike another dog. But this is very common in older dogs that have been acting this way all their life. Julia's aggression was well established and there wasn't going to be an overnight miracle. To expect one in such a case is very unrealistic. Training, as explained earlier, doesn't change a dog's character or brain patterns; it just reinforces new connections, shapes new responses and redirects a dog's efforts.

With a lot of hard work, Julia improved dramatically. I remember the day when we took her off her long training line and Emily, with trembling hands, tried to find a treat in her bum-bag without success. But Julia appreciated the trust we had put in her and paid us back with good responses. And the progress continued from there.

She is now very carefree and loves going out for walks and making new canine friends. She hasn't gone for another dog in over a year. However, Emily is still uncomfortable with the prospect of Julia acting out again, and has decided to play it safe. All those years of acting badly has left a greater mark on her owner than on Julia herself, I believe. Emily therefore insists that at times Julia wear a muzzle when she's around dogs she's never met. Now, not only is Julia happy, as she has learned to get on with other dogs, but her owner is happy and relaxed too. They can enjoy their walks together without anxiety. Both of them have met many friends and have become an invaluable addition to our doggie community (no, she's not holding a water pistol at my head as I'm writing this) with all our many outings, parties, social gatherings and classes.

Beagles Trifford and Snowdrop

Another good example is our next case stufy Ollie, also a muzzle-wearer and a lot happier for it.

OLLIE

Ollie is an outgoing, rugged seven-year-old Yorkshire terrier-cross rescue dog. He was Celia's first dog; as she lived in a flat, she thought a small dog would be little trouble, so she sought out a Yorkie. Finally, she decided to take the plunge and rescued Ollie, with his sparkling eyes and gregarious nature, from Battersea Dogs' Home. It was love at first sight. She was told that he had no 'issues' that they knew of – he had been there only a day – but they'd found that he wasn't interested in toys.

The very first walk Ollie went out on with Celia was to the post office and he barked at everyone and everything along the way. In fact, Ollie had many issues and Celia had many big problems with her small dog. She got my number through one of my former clients, the owner of Beauty, a beautiful German shepherd, who'd been found abandoned, tied to a bench (but that's another story). Celia, Ollie and I started working together and, to Celia's credit, she worked exceptionally hard. She went to all our Saturday training classes at Sunnyhill Park and did many one-to-one sessions with me. She also went on daily walks with me as I was exercising my charges. These complimentary morning sessions were specifically designed for people with dogs like Ollie and Julia and over the years hundreds of people have joined me on these walks around Hampstead Heath.

At first Ollie was a reluctant trainee. He was his own man, and no one was going to tell him otherwise. But I gently persisted until we earned his cooperation. His transformation towards food was one of the slowest I've encountered, but old dogs do learn new tricks – and here (as is often the case) it wasn't just the dog that had a lot of learning to do.

Today Ollie is a reformed dog and has performed heelwork to music, routines in front of our students and onlookers at group classes, and at obedience displays. He goes for two-hour morning strolls around the Heath with between five and ten other graduates of our school. Their owners meet up regularly and sit down at the end of each walk for a cup of coffee at the local café. All these dogs have had problems, but it's the good side of them that we high-lighted and encouraged. Now everyone admires this happy bunch of well-behaved dogs, and I couldn't ask for a finer walking advertisement for our Hand Feeding routine.

To see Ollie, you'd think he was the happiest dog on Earth. The muzzle that Ollie has to wear at times doesn't bother him a bit and his tail is in a constant state of wagging. And you know this dog that didn't like toys? Celia discovered that using a squeaky ball was even more effective than treats for recall. He *loves* toys!

This story has more than one happy ending. Not only is Ollie a reformed dog, he has also been the instrument by which Celia has widened her social circle. But she's earned her happiness. She stuck with Ollie, sought help and figured out what Ollie needed to be the kind of dog she needed him to be. All credit to her. She's done a fine job and probably saved Ollie's life. Had she not persisted, he might have ended up back at a shelter and goodness knows what his fate would have been.

As well as being a wonderful example of a rehabilitated rescue dog, Ollie has landed himself a job! He regularly dog-sits his pal, Casper, when their owners go out. Casper still gets a bit lonely on his own sometimes but is perfectly happy if his ten-times-smaller buddy stays with him. Well done, Olls!

Sometimes it's just a matter of finding the right home for a particular dog. Not all dogs suit all people. And not all dogs like one another either. The following is a real case of experimenting and finding a solution that eventually worked for all, especially the dog.

PADDY

Paddy is a three-year-old Patterdale terrier-schnauzer cross who was rescued from Battersea Dogs' Home's shelter in Brands Hatch, Kent, by David and Sally. They had chosen him as a companion for their Patterdale, Mr Tod. Unfortunately, Paddy kept attacking Mr Tod and, in David's words, 'they fought like tigers'. With aching hearts, they took Paddy to Battersea with specific instructions on the type of home that he would be happiest in – a single-dog family – and how they thought he could be helped.

A few days later David and Lucy read about me in Trevor Grove's article in the Saturday Times. Immediately, they rang me for a session with Mr Tod and to discuss the fights he'd had with Paddy, as David still clung to hope that he might be able to take Paddy back. I said I'd be happy to help out with Paddy.

David rang up Battersea only to be disappointed to learn that Paddy had been re-homed. David wrote them a letter requesting that if Paddy was returned to the shelter in Kent, he'd appreciate having a chance to bring him to see me. As it turned out, Paddy was eventually returned to the shelter. The family that took him on called him completely 'unmanageable', and since he'd returned to Battersea, he had been biting the kennel staff. They felt that because he had been re-homed unsuccessfully several times there was a good possibility he would run out of chances. But if David wanted to give Paddy a try once more and work with me, then of course it was worth another effort. So Paddy went home with David and then came straight to me to stay for a week.

This is a service I occasionally offer clients whose dogs have very tricky problems that need extra special attention and time. As I always have a group of dogs living with me, the dogs that are in training get plenty of socialisation. And because I'm always on duty, they also get plenty of behavioural modification on a 24/7 basis. I can't claim to cure a dog in a week or two of all his problems (oh, how I wish I had a magic wand!), but I can make a lot of progress in turning a dog around to understanding what good behaviour is, and make his insight click into place in many intense situations. (Behaviourists use the term 'flooding' in this case, as the dog in training is flooded with the overpowering element that is sending him over the top – birds, horses, people in a busy park and so on – so soon the trainee doesn't get as excited as before – there's simply no point.) And, as the owners are trained in my methods, they can continue to build on the work that I've started with their dog. It can't work without the owner's dedicated participation.

After our initial meeting, David and I also discussed the possibility that Mr Tod and Paddy just didn't like each other and maybe it wasn't fair to make them live together. At times the amount of training, effort and the risks involved overwhelm the advantage of the training itself. In this case I believed separating Mr Tod and Paddy was the best thing to do. David agreed but still wanted to help Paddy, such was his affection for him.

David's daughter, Lucy, who runs a livery stable, agreed to take Paddy if he could behave himself. She had 30 horses and three other dogs to look after, so Paddy was going to have to learn how to be sociable and settle in without causing problems.

Paddy went through the Good Boy Dog School intensive training course with me. I have to confess that this isn't the easiest type of case to handle, as I find it very uncomfortable being the last hope for a dog. It's a huge responsibility, but I knew that if I could make headway with Paddy, he'd be well looked after by David and his family. David felt that Paddy had been abused and that he often attacked as a way to survive. If Paddy could only learn that he could trust or rely on someone, he'd be a great companion.

I made good progress with Paddy. He happily accepted our large dog pack and met over a hundred dogs in that week with only a couple of attempts to bite some – which we were prepared for – so he didn't succeed. But, as I expected, I couldn't claim to have cured him completely of his fighting habit in one week. Much to my embarrassment, when David and Lucy came to collect Paddy, he had a go at another dog. Still, I gave Paddy a good report card. I felt he was progressively getting the message of what was good and what was bad behaviour, and what was expected of him. I gave David and Lucy specific instructions on how to keep him in line. He had settled well into my home and I felt Paddy really had a chance if Lucy kept after him.

But Lucy felt he was more than she was going to be able to handle, so David kept Mr Tod and Paddy separated for a few days while he struggled to figure out what to do with Paddy. To his credit, he was determined to sort out Paddy and give him a good home. When Paddy wasn't fighting, he was a great dog and David felt it a terrible injustice for him to go.

Suddenly Paddy's luck took a turn for the better. On Lucy's livery stable there is a farm cottage inhabited by four young men who all work in the agricultural business. One of these was brought up with a Patterdale and was keen to have one of his own now that he had left home.

And so Paddy was brought to his new home with specific instructions on how to handle his aggressive nature. Paddy has now been in his new home for over a year. He's settled down well and has even found a job! He's a champion ratter, welcomed on all local farms for his ability to clear rats out of feed sheds. And, he's also made friends. He plays with Lucy's young Jack Russell and goes down the pub with the lads most evenings.

Thanks to David's persistence, Paddy has a wonderful new life – probably better, David admits, than if he'd stayed with him. It's a story with a happy ending – not the one David had originally anticipated when he first laid eyes on Paddy, but a great ending nonetheless.

Humbert

HAMISH AND HAGGIS

Before we wrap up, I wish to leave you with a story about one of my friends and Good Boy Dog School graduates. Hardly a day goes by when I don't run into Lady Jane Elisabeth Garland and the waggedy tails of her springer spaniels, Hamish and Haggis, as they emerge together from the paths on the Heath. I admire many dog handlers, both professional and amateur, but Jane is one of my favourites. She has had several dogs over the years, not just springers, and had never had any formal training before she and I met, though she has always tried to build on her knowledge with every dog she has owned. Because of her consistent and persistent learning and her admirable ambition, she is one of the most effective handlers I know.

You should see Hamish and Haggis in action. Just recently I had a one-to-one training session with a springer puppy, Mazy, and her owner, Ali, when Jane and her 'boys' stopped to say hello. We were treated to a wonderful demonstration where Jane first threw two dummies in opposite directions, then had each dog run halfway towards them, where she asked them to stop. Then she asked Hamish to go for the dummy that Haggis had been on his way to, and Haggis to go after the dummy that Hamish had been going towards – so that they passed by each other. They dutifully picked up their toys, ran back to Jane and adopted perfect 'present' positions.

This sounds rather easy to do but in truth it requires a considerable amount of practice to achieve a consistent level of accuracy. Jane and her boys practise every day when they are out walking, which helps them prepare for when they go out on shoots, and I often ask them to perform something new, unexplored and unprepared when I have the great fortune to bump into them. Do they ever fail? Only at times and with a very low rate of errors, all of which are very easy to master after only a single repeat. Jane is well equipped with more skill and knowledge to deal with any new challenge, as the next one is always easier than the one before.

This is precisely the way she has mastered obedience training: by continually giving her dogs new challenges, not the same old thing time after time. In this way they are able to develop their knowledge, as well as broaden their generalisation abilities. She also doesn't let them slack off, as she knows it's a fast downward trend into disorder if she does. Instead, working and playing with her dogs is something she knows she has to persist at every day for the lifetime of each of her dogs, although it may only require one or two minutes of practice out of an hour's walk.

Jane's achievements would be extraordinary without the additional circumstance of Haggis having been born with a serious genetic disorder that affects his bones. Like most of his bloodline, he broke both his front legs, at different times, in freak accidents – walking down stairs and running along a footpath. He had to be confined for a great length of time in order that his bones could heal. For such an active dog, both mentally and physically, this could have been a terrible defeat. But Jane kept up his mental exercises with food challenges, clicker training and hands-off free shaping. Now she can talk to him just as if he were a human being, such is his mental acumen. He's just like any human being in her household, with the same brains, reactions, responsibilities and capabilities –

maybe even more so! He is the quintessential dream pet, and so can yours be if you have the same amount of ambition that Jane has demonstrated.

It is such a pleasure to meet up with Jane and Hamish and Haggis, and I can't describe how delightful it is to work with these two fine dogs, even if it's just for a few moments once in a while. For me to see their skill and continued progress is one of my greatest rewards. It makes my life's work all worthwhile.

Training never ends – and this is why it is both a challenge and a joy. Just as many of us never want to stop learning, our dogs are thirsty for knowledge and new experiences. I hope that you, just like Jane, have been bitten by the training bug and continue to build on your education with your dog, and all the dogs that will grace your life.

CONCLUSION

My little dog – a heartbeat at my feet.
Edith Wharton

Congratulations! You're now a graduate of the Good Boy Dog School. You've gained a greater understanding of why dogs behave the way they do, how they think, what their motivations are and how all this can help you to communicate with your dog to be a good boy or girl. You've learned what you need to be properly prepared to train your dog, to be able to anticipate problems and to solve them in creative ways best suited to you and your companion.

You've learned that training – for all involved – is an enjoyable experience that requires your diligence and persistence. You've learned skills aplenty to train your dog to do almost anything a dog can do. Whether you just want a pet who will be well behaved, or one that you can take all the way to the top of competitions, you've learned the essential groundwork, as well as much of the advanced tools you require to be well on your way.

I knew you could do it. Now, stop reading, fill up a bag with treats, grab a ball, put on your shoes and all your outdoor gear, hook up your dog, and off you go. I wish you many wonderful years with your faithful companions – all your current and future ones.

I hope I'll see you around, and if you find yourself walking on Hampstead Heath, please join me and show me all you and your dog have accomplished together. In the meantime, happy training!

> *With eye upraised in his master's look to scan,*
> *The joy, the solace, and the aid of man:*
> *The rich man's guardian and the poor man's friend,*
> *The only creature faithful to the end.*
> George Crabbe, 'Faithful'

ACKNOWLEDGEMENTS

We would like to thank the following for their great contributions to the success of this book from its inception to its completion:

All my Good Boy Dog School canine trainees and graduates, and their loving and responsible owners.

The many great dog (and other animal) trainers whose tips and hints have helped me on countless occasions and have added to my overall understanding of dog behaviour.

Trevor Grove, for his kind words on the Good Boy Dog School in the Saturday *Times* and his charming book *One Dog and His Man*.

Alan Brooke, our editor, for *finding* us, and for his boundless enthusiasm for our project.

I also wish to thank my family – Anna, Nick and Kyrill – who looked after me so well when I took time off from my family duties to write this book.

BIBLIOGRAPHY

Bunk, S., 'Market Emerges for Use of Human Drugs on Pets', *Scientist*, 13 (8):1, 12 April 1999

Burch, M.R., PhD, and Bailey, J.S., PhD, *How Dogs Learn*, Howell Reference Books, 1999

Donaldson, J., *The Culture Clash: A Revolutionary New Way of Understanding the Relationship between Humans and Domestic Dogs*, James & Kenneth Publishers, 1996

——, *Dogs Are from Neptune*, Lasar Multimedia Productions, Inc., 1998

Dunbar, Dr I., *How to Teach a New Dog Old Tricks*, James & Kenneth Publishers, 1996

——, *Dog Behaviour*, Howell Book House, 1999

——, *Before You Get Your Puppy*, James & Kenneth Publishers, 2001

Elliot, J., and Ludlow, M., 'Rising tide of divorce rains cats and dogs on animal shelters', *Sunday Times*, 5 October 2003

Fisher, J., *Think Dog!: An Owner's Guide to Canine Psychology*, Cassell 2003

Lloyd, P., Mayes, A., Manstead, A.S.R., Meudell, P.R., and Wagner, H.L., *Introduction to Psychology: An Integrated Approach*, Fontana Press, 1986

Mugford, Dr R., 'Separation Anxiety', lecture, Wag and Bone Show, Ascot Racecourse, Berkshire, 16 August 2003

Neville, P., *Dog Behaviour Explained*, Parragon Publishing, 1991

O'Farrell, B., *Philosophy Dog: The Art of Loving with Man's Best Friend*, Rizzoli Publications, 2001

O'Farrell, V., *Manual of Canine Behaviour*, British Small Animal Veterinary Association, 1992

Parker, J., 'The Separation Summit', lecture, University of Warwick, 17 April 1999

Pryor, K., *Don't Shoot the Dog!: The New Art of Teaching and Training*, Bantam Books, 1999

Reid, P.J., PhD, *Excel-Erated Learning: Explaining How Dogs Learn and How Best to Teach Them*, James & Kenneth Publishers, 1996

Roberts, M., *Join-Up: Horse Sense for People*, HarperCollins, 2000

Rogerson, J., *Be Your Dog's Best Friend*, Popular Dogs, 1992

White, A., *Dog Training Instructor's Manual*, Rainbow Publishing, 2000

Whyte, P., *Living with an Alien*, Hans Kirsten Publishers Pty Ltd, 1994

Wilkes, G., *Behavior Sampler*, C&T Publishing, 1994

ABOUT THE ILLUSTRATOR

Veronika Kantorovich

Nika Kantorovich was born in 1989 in Riga, Latvia (the former USSR) and from the age of three has aspired to be an artist. Animals have always been a favourite subject – horses in particular – although since illustrating this book and attending Good Boy Summer Dog Boot Camp, dogs have also become one of her most beloved subjects.

Nika is currently at Townley Grammar School for Girls and she takes private lessons in drawing and painting, studying watercolour, oil and acrylic and classical pencil drawing. She plans to study to become a veterinary surgeon.

PICTURE CREDITS

Thanks to the following people for kindly giving permission for the use of their photographs:

Pages x; 165
Reproduced courtesy of Tim Rose, *Dogs Today* Magazine

Pages viii; 98; 217; 229
Masha Shaverneva

John Lillington

Steven Blackman

Jurga Galvanauskaite, InfoCentre

Alba Modiano

Good Boy Dog School

Positive about dogs, positive about people

GBDS is a registered Dog Training School that promotes the idea of responsible dog ownership, provides behavioural help and advice to people and families with dogs, gives dogs a good start in life, and tries to improve the lives of dogs with behavioural problems.

Run by **Dima Yeremenko**, MSc, Russian dog training instructor and behaviourist, our school offers the whole range of services, including one-to-one training and advice sessions, indoor and outside group training classes, home visits, residential training courses, obedience displays and demonstrations, and dog-walking and -minding services etc. We run regular training classes for the local RSPCA Centre and the local council in North West London. We also specialise in dog modeling/ casting work as the School has the largest number of dogs trained both for studio work and outdoor filming.

Our most popular event is the annual Dog Training Boot Camp where people live and train in a highly varied environment, and includes horse-riding, clay-pigeon shooting, seaside and river walks, and parties and banquets.

There are two other dog training instructors working at the School. With the use of our individual training methods and techniques to form dogs' positive attitude, we are able to provide for most of your dog's needs and to resolve most of its problems in a natural and stimulating environment. A large part of our new recruits are those 'difficult' dogs that have not been fortunate enough to establish stress-free, safe and enjoyable relationships with either owners or other people or animals.

By providing both theoretical and practical help and assistance, we are improving the lives of dogs from as young as eight weeks to 17-year-old veteran trainees. Old dogs can learn new tricks! But more importantly – so can you.

We publish a newsletter released every three months with our news, updates, offers and events. It is sent free of charge to all those requesting it.

More information can be obtained from our website:
www.goodboydogschool.co.uk

All further details, our regular newsletter and information can be obtained from:

Dima Yeremenko
E-mail: dimadogs@hotmail.com

SOPHIE'S STORY
Raising a chimp in the family
Vince Smith

In 1990, while Vince Smith was working as a senior keeper at Chester Zoo, a newborn chimpanzee in his care was abandoned by her mother. Named Sophie, the baby chimp was taken home and hand-reared by Vince and his wife. Six months later another new baby arrived: Oliver, their son.

Sophie's Story is an enthralling account of Sophie's life, taking readers on an emotional journey through her early years in the English countryside with Vince and his family; her traumatic removal from the family she adored into a captive zoo world; her repatriation to Africa and eventual reunion with her human foster family; and, finally, her integration into a semi-wild group of chimpanzees.

At the heart of Sophie's Story is a dramatic and moving tale that will appeal to readers of all ages. Other accounts have been written about pet animals reared in people's homes, but this book is different: Sophie wasn't a pet. A highly personal narrative centred on a chimpanzee raised with human foster parents, Sophie's Story is, as a biography, unique. Describing in detail the parallel upbringing of an infant chimp and a human child, it is an inspirational story that provides fascinating insights into the nature of our closest-living relatives – and indeed ourselves.

SNARL FOR THE CAMERA
Memoirs of a wildlife cameraman
James Gray

'An enchanting book – it reminded me of early Gerald Durrell – and it gives us a rare insight into the unexpected problems, the surprising solutions, the frustrations and anxieties of a natural history cameraman.' Redmond O' Hanlon, author of Into the Heart of Borneo

James Gray has fulfilled his childhood dream of becoming a natural history cameraman; over the years, he has filmed everything from human lice (which he had to feed on his own blood) to polar bears in the arctic, anacondas in Venezuela, gorillas in Rwanda, caiman crocodiles in South America, elephants in Thailand, and pandas in China.

In this highly entertaining and informative narrative, the author describes his (sometimes very scary) experiences filming wild animals – and introduces readers to some of the tricks of the trade. Keeping the television producers happy requires not only an inordinate amount of patience and perseverance, wading through swamps or squatting in trees for days on end – but may also require giving nature a helping hand.

This delightfully funny and eye-opening book – enhanced with superb colour photographs – is the perfect gift for anyone who enjoys wildlife programmes.